MW01048322

In the Shadow
of
God's Hand

By Diane McMillan

Cover Design: Laura Masterson

Front Cover and Back Cover Photographs by Laura Masterson
Church of Santa Maria del Mar, Barcelona, Spain

Also available:
"The Countryside Book of Verse,"
"Whimsy, Dreams and Laughter,"
"God Likes Poetry, Too!"
"Cookies, Kids and Toys"
"Horse Feathers and Old Lace"
and "Down the Back Lane"
by Diane McMillan

ISBN-13: 978-1511999540

ISBN-10: 1511999543

Rest, Weary Traveller

Tired feet shuffle
Another mile,
Oh, weary soul,
Come rest awhile.

Come to the table
Where you can sup,
Partake of God's meal
And be lifted up.

Here at God's table,
Drink the new wine
Eat of the bread
That is sublime.

Rest, weary traveller,
Away from all strife,
Come to God's table
In search of new life.

Come, be refreshed,
Revived anew,
Filled with God's Spirit
Flooding over you.

Rest, weary traveller,
Come in from the cold,
Be filled with God's love –
That's purer than gold.

Rest, weary traveller,
So you can sing
This new song of life
That Jesus can bring.

On Being Useful

Lord, thank You
For the time I have
To come on bended knee
And lift a prayer up to You
For setting this sinner free.

Can You help my dearest friend
Get through another day,
Fill her with compassion
And teach her how to pray?

Lord, give me direction
On what I ought to say
To those who have strayed
And have lost their way?

Then give me more wisdom,
Help me to understand
The needs and the pain
Of my fellow man.

Lord, make me aware –
More useful I'll be
To offer up help
For the hurt that I see.

At end of the day,
When all is done,
I can thank You, Lord,
For each victory won.

Oh, that I
More useful can be,
To You, my Lord
Who first saved me.

Road to Reality

Does the "Road of Reality"
Call to you,
When you least expect it
From out of the blue?

Does it beckon to you
And call out your name?
Does it promise you riches
And wonderful fame?

Do you long to go
Where others have been,
To search for adventure
You have not seen?

Or do you look
The other way,
And wish you could
Go there some day?

Does the grass growing
On the other side
Look greener to you
Than the places you hide?

Are you happy
With the life you live
Or do you wonder
If there's more to give?

Are you content
To stay where you are,
Never to see mysteries
Scattered so far?

Whenever you decide
What you should do,
Then pray to the Lord –
He will guide you.

A Donkey Sings

Little donkey, sing your prayer
In evening's dying light,
Sing to Jesus up above,
Your song of coming fright.

The years have quickly passed
Since that glorious day,
When you anxiously carried
Jesus Christ this way.

Sing that prayer of reverence,
Beneath branches high,
Well is it any wonder
We hear the donkey cry?

Now we understand
Your raspy cry of pain
Deep within your heart
You know Christ comes again.

Little donkey, sing your prayer
For this world to hear,
Now you've told us plainly
Christ is drawing near.

Little donkey, sing that prayer,
God holds you in His Hand,
As we listen with delight
To the echo across the land.

Through a Child's Eyes

So far removed
From troubled things
That growing up
So normally brings.

From common goals
Or prayers at table,
Of bedtime stories
And other fables.

Now we've grown
Old and grey,
Those childhood memories
Seem to fade away.

Hearts grow troubled
Our minds fill with doubt,
As we see the turmoil
All about.

Were we blind
And could not see
The world's problems
At age of three?

Or do they seem
Through children's eyes
Less of a threat –
We can only surmise.

When here
On glory seat I sit,
Trying hard to remember
And not to fret.

So thank You, Lord,
For hearing me,
As with remorse
I cry to Thee.

Inspiration

Inspiration comes
From life's every woe,
Maybe you lost a friend
Or have a throbbing toe.

We can be inspired
Dreaming 'neath a tree,
While watching the toil
Of a little honey bee.

Or when you see your breath
Some cold and frosty day,
Of spring beauties flowering
In the month of May.

Maybe it's a cricket
Singing after dark,
Or a woodpecker pounding
On rigid tree bark.

Was it your little cat
Resting in your lap?
Or while you tried to read
A tattered road map?

Do you take inspiration
From famous people
Or was it when you came to pray
'Neath the old church steeple?

Did you read a book
And did it inspire you?
A wrenching sad story
Of what people have gone through?

Do your little children
Playing in the yard,
Inspire you a lot
And make you work hard?

Does the story of Jesus
Hanging on the Cross,
Inspire you to pray
And thank God for His loss?

God's Handiwork

Watch the brown cow
Walk through the pasture,
With her young calf
Following after.

See the old horse
With stripe on her face,
Stand in the shade
As her colt raced.

Down in the barnyard
A flock of red hens,
Scratch in the dirt
With chicks from the pens.

See these mothers
With babies in tow,
Show us creation
And things we don't know.

All of these lessons
Taught at a young age,
Show us the world
Is just a big stage.

Come, learn of life
And hardship too,
Come see God's handiwork –
It will teach you.

See clouds in the sky,
Stars and the moon,
The sun and the rain
And snow that comes soon.

All that God's done
For granted we take,
Do we say, "Thank You"
For what He did make?

Graciousness

Raised in a dingy apartment
Over a Hardware Store,
He never learned to talk
Until he was twenty-four.

Blind in both eyes,
Couldn't read or write,
When his mother died,
He was sick with fright.

See the little boy
In the wheelchair,
Both legs are gone –
Such a look of despair.

Why do I cry out?
I shouldn't complain!
There is nothing wrong with me –
No illness and no pain.

I bow my head in prayer
Thanking You for Your grace,
*"Lord, teach me to help
This suffering human race.*

*Help me to do what I can –
Whether some time or prayer,
Teach me to give to others
And be thankful they are there."*

The Sting of Death

Sometimes when sadness
Grips our hearts,
We cannot pray,
Lord, how do we start?

Dear Father, we reach out,
Our minds are so blue –
It's difficult
To speak to you.

We ask for Your comfort
And loving grace,
The death of a loved one
Consumes every space.

We feel so alone,
Just like Your Son
When there on the cross
He finally hung.

Forgive us dear Father
For crying to Thee
When Your only Son
Died on the tree.

Turn pain into praise,
Remorse into song –
So in death, we can try
To right all of our wrongs.

A Grandmother in Prayer

Alone she sat,
Head bowed in prayer –
No movement came
From her rocking chair.
What caught my eye –
For I could see
Those frail old hands
Clasped on her knee.
Fingers entwined,
Wrinkled by age,
That posture of prayer,
When mind is engaged.

A habit from years,
Not forced at all,
Her talk with God,
I clearly recall.
The words of praise
So lovingly said
Like visiting an old friend
Is what she did,
Her face lit up
As if it glowed
When softly she spoke –
The praises flowed.

So there she sat
In her favourite chair
With head bowed low
In humble prayer.

Filling a Need

It happens to us
When life goes bad,
Down in our hearts,
We grow very sad,
We see no sunshine,
The joy fades away –
There is no gladness
In us today.

This is the time
We seek out our Friend –
Bow heads in prayer,
Come talk to Him.
He knows our concerns,
What we're going to say
But it needs talking over
So come and pray.

Don't put it off
And toy with fate,
Talk to our Saviour
Before it's too late.
The answer will come
It may take a few days,
Be patient with God
And be constant in praise.

Prayer at Daybreak

Heavenly Father,
Help me today
To walk in Your Spirit
And be filled with
Your saving grace.
Control the things I say
And the actions of my mind.
I ask for Your joy
In all my conversations

And for Your direction
In all decisions made.
Give me patience, Lord,
And honest sincerity
In every task undertaken
In my life today.
I give You all praises,
Honour and glory
In Jesus' name.

Amen

In Search of God's Love

I constantly prayed
In a stubborn way,
Not willing to let go
Of wrong things I say.

Getting frustrated
And very cast down
It felt like I was
Not gaining ground.

Then one day
Up against the wall
I cried out to God
To take it all!

"Take it away!"
I let out a shout,
"Remove this burden!"
I cried out.

Thank You, oh, Father
For things I say
And thank You for listening
When I bow to pray.

I thank God for Calvary,
The blood on the cross
And for helping this sinner
Who was once lost.

A feeling of joy
Came into my soul,
I finally gave in,
That was the Lord's goal.

Give it all up,
Now I can see –
Believe in His comfort,
It will set you free.

Three In One

Every time I stumble,
You pick me up again,
Lord, don't You ever tire
Of things I do in vain?

I know of Your forgiveness,
First hand I learned from You –
You answer every prayer
When I am so blue.

The thing I most admire
Is Your spiritual grace
Following after Jesus
Just to take His place.

For now I'm not alone,
The Trinity leads me
And every problem I face
Is now solved by three.

You win my losing battles
And never leave my side,
From Your loving friendship,
I have no need to hide.

Thank You, Lord, for patience
And all-consuming love,
Thank You now for listening
From Your throne above.

Footsteps on Sand

I followed in God's footsteps
Across the burning sand
And stared upon the water
Divided by His hand.

I looked upon the water
Of the stormy sea
As Jesus reached out to Peter
When he cried to Thee.

I saw the saddened faces
Grieving at Cavalry's tree,
For the nail-pierced Hands
That had set us free.

At the empty tomb,
I heard the worried prayer
Whispered out by Mary
Because You weren't there.

I stumbled down the dusty roads
Walking all alone
Crying out in sorrow
To Your heavenly throne.

I know that You hear me
In my hours of grief
For the burden is lifted
And I feel relief.

Thank You, Lord, for caring
And for the stories told
As Your wandering sheep
Return to Your loving fold.

Detours

On the road of life,
So perilous today,
We ask You, Lord,
To lead the way.

Guide us now
With Your Hand
Through stormy detours
Created by man.

Smooth the roughness
In our lives
That prevents us seeing
Through clear eyes.

Take the hatefulness
In our hearts today
And wash our sins
And troubles away.

Encourage our faith
To flourish and grow
From the heavenly seed
You lovingly sow.

Lift us up
When we fall down
Help us to walk
On level ground.

Continue to feed
Your hungry sheep
So we grow up in grace
And do not weep.

Thank You for hearing
Our humble prayer,
We know Your Spirit
Is watching here.

Help us to conquer
The stormy deep
That prevents minds
From restful sleep.

We sing out to You
With glorious praise,
In hymns of thanksgiving,
Our voices we raise.

Encompassing Love

I learned how much God cared
When at the tomb I cried
For the savage way
That our Saviour died.

This God whose love is boundless
As deep as any sea,
Gave His only Son
That we would all be free.

Now I bow in prayer
My heart is humble, too,
And ask that You accept me
For whatever I can do.

Help us understand
Your encompassing love
And the reason that You sent it
To us from above.

Are You Still There?

Angels fly
Through timeless deep
As the dead in Christ
Rest in eternal sleep.

I hear the voices
Of men in prayer
Calling out to God,
"Are You still there?"

"Are You still there?"
Hear our cry
When innocent children
Are about to die.

"Are You still there?"
When with a shout,
We sing in joy
And yell it out.

"Are You still there?"
When we fear
Over the future –
It causes a tear.

For I am sure
That You're still there
When asked in faith,
You answer prayer.

I am sure
That You're around
When new churches are built
On hallowed ground.

For I know
When day is done
And we bow in thanksgiving
Life's battles are won.

Talents

In Jesus' time,
The talents spent
Were people's money
Bartered, traded and leant.

On the other hand,
Talents could be
Those inward gifts
Used by you and me.

We all have talents,
Sometimes not seen,
Hidden away,
Where they have been.

All of these talents,
Though great or small,
Should be used
For the good of all.

If your special talent
Is used only by you –
Then happily share it
With others, too.

Be it a painting,
A gift or a card,
Maybe some groceries
Or help in the yard.

It doesn't take much
To spread talents around
And help out a person
When they are down.

Gifts From God

Sitting on a chair
In the backyard,
I looked around
Really hard
And I could see
What God has done
Providing for all
And not missing one.
Birds flying with babies
Up in the trees,
A horse in a paddock
In grass to his knees,
The smell of fresh hay
Cut out in the field,
A snail on a flower
With his shell for a shield.
Precious wee moments
Out in the sun –
Gifts from the Lord
That make life such fun.
Take time to sit back,
To soak it all in,
Then bow your head
And give thanks to Him.
What more could we want
On this journey through life
Than what God has provided
Free of all strife?
Come offer up glory
And humble praise
For God's wondrous gifts
Showered on us today.

Lessons of Life

We struggle with her illness
And all wonder why
This had to happen –
It makes us all cry.
What lesson in life
Are we to learn
That causes this sadness
And makes us so stern?
What sadness we suffer,
The heartache we bore,
When a young man died
His soul burdened and sore.
The sin of all man
Was heavy on God's mind
But no anger He carried,
Not any could we find.
Those lessons in life,
The answers unseen
And search as we do,
Might just be a dream.
Perhaps we aren't looking
In the right place
And all that we need
Is a little more grace,
Served up by the Master
In a helping of love
That He sends from His throne
In the heavens above.

Finding Peace

You can rest briefly
In the Hand of God,
Then walk transfigured
Where others have trod.

You can raise voices
In joyful praise
For how you have changed
Over these days.

You can bow down
In humble prayer
Or walk away
As if you don't care.

The road that you take
May be rough and steep
But God will go with you,
There safely to keep.

Seek joy in your heart
And peace of mind
As with the Saviour,
His glory you find.

Don't pass Him by
Don't walk away,
Spend time with the Lord
And be at peace today.

Road of Life

The road of life
Is rough and broken,
Many harsh words
You will hear spoken.

Be not dismayed
Or overwhelmed,
God is steering,
He's at the helm.

Let Him take control
Oh, walk hand in hand,
Don't think you're alone
In a strange land.

Come often in prayer
To His mercy seat
Don't answer to evil
And go down in defeat.

For God has chosen
The way you should go
Don't think you're alone
And that He doesn't know.

The road is not easy
You travel today,
He will be with you –
You won't go astray.

The Sound of Footsteps

Footsteps crossed softly
On old wooden floor
Then paused briefly
To go out the door.
Footsteps hurried early
To the kitchen stove
Cooking up porridge
For a hungry drove.
Footsteps stumbled blindly
Down a back alley
As homeless old drunk
Tried hard to rally.
Footsteps walked quickly
Down busy hall
As doctor rushed on
Making a call.
Footsteps, they paused
Out at the grave
Where a young body lay
Nobody could save.
Footsteps pass time
In old rocking chair
As senior stares out
With a look of despair.
Footsteps, they struggle
Up Calvary's hill,
Lugging this cross
Was His Father's will.
Footsteps go quietly
Down the church hall
As sinner now answers
This alter call.

Spiritual Filling

Lord, when we anguish,
Don't know what to say,
Send down Your Spirit
And help us to pray.

Feed us and guide us
With Your loving Hand –
We bow in reverence
Like any humble man.

Teach us to be thankful
In words that are true
Surmounting our failures
To call upon You.

Take our stubborn pride
And lock it away,
Increase joy and grace
In our hearts as we pray.

Make us and mould us
In all that we do
So our prayers and praises
Travel easily to You.

Complete Love

Come accept God
And His complete love,
Be showered with grace
From His throne above.

When trials befall you,
You're burdened and sore,
Lift prayers in faith
And be changed evermore.

Rejoice in His peace,
Tell Him you care,
Walk in God's presence –
He is always there.

For He will guide you
From His high tower,
Be filled with these blessings
And feed from His power.

This plan is so simple
So come and explore
To be filled with His grace –
Just knock at His door.

Empty Tomb

Oh, empty tomb,
We cry aloud
Where sadly lays
The snow white shroud.
Our Saviour gone –
No more to rest
Among the dead,
That was His test.
We cry real tears
And bow our heads
Afraid to whisper
"He is not dead."
Oh, empty tomb,
See our surprise
For not understanding
What's before our eyes.
With broken hearts
We laid you here
Now we've returned
And you've disappeared.
Oh, empty tomb,
We cry out to thee,
Our Lord now taken,
He is set free.
Not comprehending
Our inner fears,
We bow our heads
And weep these tears.

Joy In My Heart

There is nothing
Left to say
For life's been rewarding
Each and every day.

So when I go,
My feet leave this ground,
All you will hear
Is a joyful sound.

I'll not complain
Nor will I cry
When finally comes
My turn to die.

I've done more than most
Stood on mountaintops,
Then shopped in stores
Until I could drop.

I've seen the ocean
And deep canyon floor
Walked through a forest
To a hidden lakeshore.

So when all is done,
Nothing is left to do,
I'll go my own way
And not bother you.

The poems are all written,
No books left to do –
Just joy in my heart
For knowing You.

I'll look into the sky
So far from harm
And walk with my Lord
Leaning on His arm.

Hallelujah Breakdown

You know what it's like
To have a hallelujah breakdown
When everything in life
Makes you feel the clown.

Blame it on the weather –
Maybe just the day,
Nothing will go right
No matter what you say.

Now isn't that just human,
Don't shed any tears
For the Lord can help you
Wash away your fears.

Perhaps you prayed for patience,
Thought you'd have your way,
Then all hell broke loose
At the start of day.

Be careful what you ask for
'Cause God hears your pleas,
You may not be prepared
Down there on your knees.

When things have a way
Of getting out of hand,
You'd better go in prayer
To that heavenly Man.

Ask Him for guidance,
Be careful what you say
For He will fill your needs
When, in faith, you pray.

Words

Painful words
So timidly spoken,
We pray to You
When hearts are broken.

Words of joy
And glorious praise,
Voices of gratitude,
We happily raise.

Words of regret
When harsh phrases are spoken,
Sometimes it's too late
For this half-hearted token.

Words of forgiveness
Down on bent knees
So humbly expressed
And passed up to Thee.

These words of love
Sent in faithful prayer
Telling You, Father,
We really do care.

Backup

Rabble rousers
They were called,
For they spoke their thoughts
To men out loud.

Courageous disciples
Who showed no fear,
Not scared of death,
They shed no tear.

God was with them,
He'd back them up,
They'd sat with Jesus –
Drank from His cup.

Those days are past,
Now they are gone
For man has forgotten
He can do no wrong.

A time of judgment
Will come to all
So be prepared
To answer that call.

Oh, walk with the Lord,
Both day and night,
Don't wander away
Out of His sight.

Be Not Afraid

On the road of life,
I thought I was stumped
But praying to God
Got me over the hump.

No money for groceries
Causes a frown,
The trials of life
Can wear us down.

Sometimes our lives
Stop with a thump
But faith in our Father
Gets us over the bump.

Be not afraid
He will pick us up,
Come to the Master –
Drink from His cup.

No problem is given
That we cannot bear
For it is written
Our Lord God will share.

We struggle in daylight
On the hot sand
And conquer rough waters
By God's calming hand.

When the trials of life
Beckon out to you
Remember our Saviour
Will carry us through.

An Ode to Violet

A farmer's wife is what she was,
I remember well,
Stop and have a cup of tea,
Sit and visit a spell.

Busy with chores,
Working at home,
Cooking and laundry,
Sweeping with broom.

Life it was busy,
Get kids off to school,
Start baking pies –
No time to fool.

If there was a problem,
Vi would be right there
With a batch of cookies
And to say a prayer.

Play the piano
If there was a need,
Quilt with the ladies
With lightning quick speed.

Supplement income
With a little job,
Pride it was justified
In the sight of our God.

Grandchildren came
To sit on her lap –
Rock them to sleep,
A good place to nap.

After the farm
It was hard to slow down,
Deliver Meals on Wheels
All about town.

Help out at the church,
Her soup I can taste
Made with loving care
And never in haste.

Hands always working,
The years they slip by,
Busy with family –
That was our Vi.

Now she won't suffer,
Kids don't you cry,
For we see her smiling
Up there on high.

Caught up with Donald
To rest with the Lord,
That was Violet's intention
And her final word.

Green Hill

I found a green hill
Not too far away
Early every morning
I climb it to pray.

There I can talk
With no one around,
Speak with my Father
Up on the high ground.

Pray for forgiveness
From all of my sins,
Ask that He cleanse me
Deep down within.

I found a green hill
Where I feel at ease
To talk to the Lord
Down on my knees.

A green hill of solace,
Away I can steal,
Bathed in God's Spirit,
My soul it can heal.

Do you have a green hill,
A place you can stay
To share all of your problems
When you go to pray?

Thanksgiving

Thunder and rain,
North wind and snow,
Hailstones and lightning,
The storms they will blow.

Humidity and heat,
Ground is baked dry,
Everything's turned brown
It does make us cry.

Animals hunt for shade
'Cause they pant in the sun
But life must go on
Even though it's no fun.

I'm sad, oh, so sad,
To see it like this
But God never promised
It all would be bliss.

From trials grow patience
Through strife healing rain,
You feel you might suffer
But it isn't in vain.

For God will uphold us
When we faithfully pray
And give our thanksgiving
For this wonderful day.

Words of Thanksgiving

In the dawn,
I come to say
What's on my mind
And thankfully pray
To You, oh, Lord,
I call Your Name
Because of Jesus,
Life is not the same.

You pick me up
When I am down
And give me a smile
To replace each frown,
You gave me strength
When I was weak
And shone Your light
When I took a peek.

You walk with me
Through miry clay
And encourage me,
Good things to say.
Oh, Father God,
I sing Your praise
With a joyful heart,
My voice will raise.

Hear these words
I sing to Thee
For Your saving grace
From my bent knee.

Too Late to Cry

The cupboard is empty,
The table so bare,
We are too busy
To bow in prayer.
Our gas tanks are empty,
No fuel for the fire,
No faith in our hearts
Is like no air in a tire.
Why are we lonely,
So hungry and cold
When there are no prayers
Sent to God so bold?
No words of thanksgiving,
We ignore You,
Life is complicated
We don't know what to do.
No prayers of repentance
Or stories of old,
No searching for God
That's like purest gold.
We cry out in anguish,
In the dark we are lost,
Not counting our blessings
Or the price of the cross.
Call out in reverence,
Speak to the Lord,
Ask Him for forgiveness
His Son shall be adored.
No drink of water,
The well has run dry
When will we all learn –
It's too late to cry?

The Door

I hear Jesus tapping
On my broken heart's door,
He's coming to forgive me
Not to settle the score.

Afraid to let Him come in,
I cautiously turn to pray...
Forgive this tired old sinner
Before Jesus turns away.

A much greater Power
Makes me open the door,
Regaled in His splendour
Jesus crosses the floor.

I bow in humbleness –
There are no words to say,
For I opened up the door
So Jesus could come to stay.

Now He dwells in my heart,
Life's trials seem much less
And I must admit
That I'm rich and blessed.

Letting Go

When asking forgiveness
We should know
In our guilty minds
To let it go.

God hears our prayer
And truthful plea –
Just let it go
And leave it be.

But we hang on
Or so it seems,
Those guilty feelings
Cloud our dreams.

God has forgiveness,
Don't lose sight –
Just let it go,
Overcome your fright.

We win the battle
When in fear,
We bow and ask,
He dries each tear.

So pray in thanksgiving,
God's love will show
When in our hearts,
We let it go.

The Least We Can Do

Together we call
And cry out to Thee
Hear this request
Coming from bent knee.

We give You the glory,
Loving grace do we seek,
Not for ourselves
But those who are weak.

We pray for the sick,
For hearts full of shame
And for the innocent
Who shoulder the blame.

May there be blessings
For those with no home
And hope for the suffering
Who wander alone?

Help for the hungry
And people who thirst
But Lord heal the children
For they should come first.

Will there be a time
When man's needs are met,
That the burden is lifted
And we don't have to fret?

But don't get us wrong,
It's the least we can do –
Bow down in prayer
And lift needs to You.

The Way

Lord, ease the worry
That creases our brow,
Send Your grace
To feed us now.

When in the dark,
We lose our way,
Light the path
We take today.

Lord, when life's trials
Increase our tears,
Send Your Spirit
To comfort our fears.

We ponder which road
That we should go,
So thank You, Father,
For You already know.

When in sadness,
We think all is lost,
Remind us of Jesus
And the price of the cross.

Father God,
We come Your way
With grateful hearts
To bow and pray.

Pay Up

If we had to pay
To ask a prayer,
Would any be sent
To God up there?

What would the price be
For each time we cussed
And selfishly raised
A temperamental fuss?

I might not talk
Or speak out loud
For fear of what
Sails to the clouds.

No, I'd rather pay
Whatever the price
To bow in prayer
And say it nice.

For we know
The ransom call
That Jesus paid
For us all.

Majesty and Grace

Heavenly Father,
We rejoice in the presence
Of Your glory
And remain humble
In the fullness of Your grace.
Our voices sing
Praises and gratitude
For the blessings
Poured out by Your love.
Lord, hear these songs of adoration
That come from rejoicing hearts.
Father God, continue to shower
Your abiding peace upon us
As we strive to increase
Our devotion and thanksgiving
To Your majesty and love,
In Jesus' name, we pray.

Amen

Heaven's Crown

Lord, upon our heads,
You place heaven's crown
And lift us up
When we fall down.
You wipe the tears
From mournful eyes
And stop to listen
To our cries.
As innocent children,
We come to Thee,
Searching for love
And Your sympathy.

Those outstretched Arms
Welcome us home,
No longer to struggle
And walk all alone.
On humble knees,
We come to say
Thank You, Jesus,
For loving us this way.
Glory we give
And blessings we take,
Not just from God
But for our own sake.

Unconditional Love

The prodigal children
All stray from home
Through unchartered waters,
They will now roam.
We quietly pray
And ask God above
To send them a measure
Of unconditional love.
Ask that He watch them,
Keep them from harm,
Walk there beside them
With an outstretched arm.

Don't cry out in anger
Although we feel pain,
An unforgiving heart
Has nothing to gain.
So welcome them home,
Don't run and hide,
Throw open the door
And stifle your pride.
Their heavenly Father,
Has forgiven them, too,
And as their parents,
It's what we should do.

In the Shadow of God's Hand

In God's Hand,
I lay my need,
All those worries,
The sin and greed.

To His throne,
I take my case
Asking of Him,
Less pain to face.

In God's presence,
I bring my fears
And wait patiently
As He dries my tears.

In God's church,
Sing out praise
And offer thanks,
His joy to raise.

On humble knees,
In heartfelt prayer,
I tell God
How much I care.

I know the love
On Calvary's tree
And what His sacrifice
Means to me.

Man of Motion

Our Man of Motion
Walked the burning sand,
Now called holy places
In a distant land.
He healed the sick
The blind and lame
Then taught on the mount
To spread the flame.
He walked on water
To Peter's surprise
And never once
Did He tell any lies.
The people came,
They listened in awe
When He spoke of the love
On which they could draw.
Our Man of Motion
Filled hungry hearts
With peace and charity
He imparts.
He spoke of a time
When He would leave
And the Spirit would come –
So do not grieve.
He fed them fishes
And manna from above
But all the while
He taught God's love.
This Man of Motion,
Oh, could it be,
His purpose on earth
Was to set us free.

Glory, Glory

Glory, glory,
Lord divine,
Heal this aching
Heart of mine,
Take the pain
You clearly see
From this life
And set me free.

Glory, glory,
Lord above,
Wash us all
With Your love.
Cleanse us from
Unwanted sin,
Come right now
To live within.

Glory, glory,
Lord of light,
Guide us through
The dark of night,
Send Your Spirit,
Light the way
As we go
About this day.

Glory, glory,
Son of God,
Bless this land
On which You've trod,
With hearts of joy,
Hear our praise
At the tomb
On which we gaze.

Glory, glory,
Eternal lamb,
Thanks for saving us
The way You can,
Give us peace,
We sing Your praise
With thankful hearts
Our voices raise.

Asking God

Heavenly Father,
We humble ourselves
At Your mercy seat,
Lifting voices of praise
And thanksgiving to You.
We ask for a filling
Of Your wisdom and peace.
Grant unto us
The patience of Your love
And a renewing of Your Holy Spirit
So we walk in Your grace
And remain humble and true
In our worship.
Strengthen us, Your people,
In the tasks we undertake every day
That our lives are an image
Of Your grace and glory.
Lord, may our songs reflect the love
That we hold in our hearts
For Your Son, Jesus Christ.
Teach us to show that
The work of our hands
Is reflective of the path we walk
In the presence of Your Holy Spirit,
To whom we offer
All honour, glory and praise.

Amen

The Struggle

Lord, why do we struggle
At Your throne of grace
When all we have to do
Is depend upon our faith?

When we bow in prayer
Down at Your alter,
Words come so hard
Oh, why do we falter?

When we ask You –
Sick and in pain,
Do we not realize
What all we can gain?

And at the cross –
Our hearts full of tears,
Your Spirit comes down
To remove our fears.

Why do we struggle
With You up above
When down upon us,
You shower Your love?

Now will the struggle
Lessen each day,
When at Your mercy seat,
We come to pray?

Redeeming Love

A day of redemption
On Calvary's tree
When our blessed Saviour
Set us all free.

That was the token
Of His pure love
Allowed by His Father
In Heaven above.

Do we thank God
For what Jesus gave
And strive to be worthy
Of the price He paid?

Come tell the story,
Sing out this song,
Of how love and glory
Keep us from wrong.

Come bow our heads
In humble prayer,
To tell our Lord Jesus
How much we care.

We care for our brothers
And those who are lost
As we bring them in prayer
To the foot of the cross.

Finding Divine Grace

Lord, I wonder
What I should say
When I bow my head
To You and pray.

Should I start
With humble praise,
Then with thankful heart,
My voice will raise?

Should I remind You
Of the good I've done
For I dare not gloat,
Boast or poke fun?

For You always know
What lays inside
From You there's nothing
That I can hide.

Here I bow
At Your mercy seat,
To offer my prayer
In words so meek.

With humble heart,
I will find
A loving Father
With grace divine.

Amen

Nature of God

The wind blows gently
Rustling the trees,
I listen intently –
Is God speaking to me?

The colours of fall
Set the woodlots ablaze
And there in the distance,
Angels sing His praise.

The heat of the summer
Burns down on me
As I hear Jesus crying
From yonder tree.

When cold winter winds
Blow down from the north
Remember John The Baptist
As he sallied forth.

Then in the greening
Of coming spring,
I stand in wonder
Of what God will bring.

The nature of God,
His presence well known,
Among each generation,
His seed will be sown.

Joyful Praise

In the presence of His grace,
We lift our voices of praise
Burning from within
Comes this fiery blaze.

Joyful voices singing,
Flying like a dove,
Hear these voices lifting
To the heavens above.

Sing the songs of Jesus
Like a lullaby,
The notes are sweetly floating
Up there in the sky.

Hear the songs of Jesus
Drifting up above,
Ringing out the story
Of His wondrous love.

Sing the songs of Jesus
Gladly sing out loud,
Sing with thankful voices
Up among the clouds.

Remember Jesus' parables
Spoken so lovingly
And how He healed the sick
Then set all mankind free.

The Unknown Request

Heavenly Father, we thank You
For the privilege of prayer,
We ask that the wisdom of Your word
Will dwell in our minds and souls.
Father, we know that You alone
Are aware of the hidden requests
That lay buried in our hearts.
We ask that You
Administer to all needs
In a precious and loving way,
Be it family, friends or neighbours.
Whether it be a burden,
Known only to You, Lord,
We understand and know
By Your infinite love and grace
That our prayers are answered
When Your children gather together
In like-mindedness and faith.

Thank You for hearing
The prayers of Your people,
We ask in Jesus name.

Amen

Glory Praises

We feel the love of Jesus
Penetrate each soul
And know our precious Saviour
Has reached His final goal.
Lift the banner of salvation
Oh, so very high
So others can rejoice
With us in the sky.

Come sing the glory praises
Written long ago,
Sing with loud rejoicing
So all the world will know
That Jesus is the King,
Who is known to all,
He is there to catch us
Whenever we might fall.

Come sing the glory praises
Learned so long ago,
The promise of our Saviour
Everywhere we go.
We won't win life's battles
Standing all alone
For the Spirit guides us
From His heavenly throne.

Struggle of David

David's psalms
Are full of pain
As he asks
Forgiveness again.

Feel the struggle
Deep within
As he wrestles
With his sin.

In the hunt
For God's grace,
David grows weary
Of the chase.

But in the evening's
Chilling air,
He knows God's love
Fills him there.

And determined,
He struggles on
With God's help
Pens many a song.

Now feel the praise
In the words he writes
As God takes command
Of David's life.

Joyful songs
The writer can play
As his Godly faith
Grows every day.

Through David's psalms,
We can be inspired
To find rest in God
When we grow tired.

God's Infinite Love

By God's infinite wisdom,
He taught me
To bow in prayer
At Calvary's tree.

In God's infinite grace,
He forgave me
And showed His love
Is absolutely free.

In God's infinite love,
He sent His Son
To pay the ransom
For the wrong done.

In God's infinite charity,
He gave to me,
Strength to run
And claim victory.

By His infinite Spirit,
Each day I pray
That through God's love
Others come His way.

Abundant Blessings

Abundant blessings
Sent from above
To all who ask
For God's love.

Receive His grace,
Can you just see –
It's free for the asking
For you and me.

Do not delay,
Oh, come today
And invite the Saviour
To come your way.

Ask in faith,
Your voices raise
Because His love
Sets hearts ablaze.

Now don't hesitate,
Do not decline,
Reach out to Jesus
And His Spirit divine.

Feel God's forgiveness
Melt your fears,
Strengthen your weakness
And wipe away tears.

Still Waters

Pools of water
Beneath distant hill
Ripple gently,
Then stand still.

Roaring water
Floods over the brim
But still water lies
Beneath the rim.

Sunlight shines,
Shimmering bright
On ponds of still water
When it is light.

Still water fills
The empty soul
And heals the body
To make one whole.

Everyone knows,
Still waters run deep
Down into our being,
There's no need to weep.

In our twilight years
When we slip away,
We'll drink still waters
At the end of the day.

Intercessory Prayer

We come with prayers of adoration
And thanksgiving, too,
Will You intercede, oh, Lord,
For those who don't love You?

Heal the broken-hearted
That lay open and so sore,
Oh, that they could know
Their pain You've already bore.

Encourage those who worry,
Are troubled and are blue,
Feed the hungry children
So they feel You love them, too.

Comfort those in mourning,
The minds that are distressed,
Strengthen those afraid to speak –
To You their tongues confess.

Take our hidden talents,
Help us, Lord, we pray
To be company for the lonely,
Show them friendship for today.

Lord, guide us to work for You,
In our own humble way
For we expect no glory
In what we share today.

Amen

Time Passes

I heard angels sing
On sabbath day
And bowed my head
To silently pray.

Was there a moment
That passed me by
When at the cross
I did not cry?

Was there a day
I forgot to say,
"Thank You, Jesus,
For coming my way?"

Was there a sabbath
When mind was hazy
And I missed church
Because I was lazy?

Was there a time,
Bowing at the cross,
I forgot to express
Love for God's loss?

I will make time
In humble love
To bow in prayer
To our Father above.

Fisherman

From the stormy
Windswept sea,
I hear our Saviour
Calling to me.

Come with nets
At evening tide
To fish the waters
Stretched out wide.

Cast your nets
Out on the sea,
Come save the souls
And set men free.

Fish the waters,
Catch the lost,
Save them all
At any cost.

For you know,
It was once you,
Caught in the net
And not passed through.

Come and fish
This night with me
To save the souls
Lost out at sea.

As Old-Time Christians

As old-time Christians,
We bow our heads to pray,
Thank You, Lord, for meeting
All of our needs today.

When many trials beset us,
We know not what to do,
So in our distress,
We can lean on You.

Lifting voices of gratefulness,
Hallowed be thy name
For like the lowly shepherds,
We have no one to blame.

Now we offer up to You,
Adoration and our praise
For walking there beside us
When worry fills our days.

As the measure of our faith
Is flowing through and through,
Then as old-time Christians,
We lift praises up to You.

Sometimes in our humanness,
We wander from the track
But in Your loving patience,
You gently lead us back.

So as old-time Christians
Who hunger for Your love,
We bow in thankful prayer
For that renewing from above.

Jesus' Struggles

Up on the mountain
In those early years,
He struggled with the devil
Amid many fears.

We saw His gentleness,
How loving was He
When He was inviting
Children onto His knee.

The questions were many
But with patience and care,
He taught the disciples
To be bold in their prayer.

Then in the garden,
Among the trees,
We hear Jesus crying
Down on His knees.

The worth of this Jesus
Can't be measured by time
For He works with His Father
Cleansing our hearts and minds.

Dewdrops

We walked the path
That Jesus took
Over sunbaked ground
Past a gurgling brook.

We saw the leper
Begging there
With a battered cup
Waving in the air.

We watched the woman
At the well
And then remembered
Her tale to tell.

On the hill
Among olive trees,
Hear the Master pray
In Gethsemane.

When we came
To that rugged cross,
Our hearts cried out –
The tragic loss.

Then to see
The tomb so bare,
Reliving the promise,
He is not there.

When we walked
That path again,
We felt the dewdrops
Of Jesus' pain.

Send to Us

We stand in awe
And ask again,
Lord, send to us
Your healing rain.

Send to us,
In hidden bower,
The filling of
Your awesome power.

Send to us,
In dark of night,
The glowing flame
Of precious light.

Please send to us,
When we ask,
Your wisdom
To complete each task.

Give to us
A little time
To remove the doubt
That clouds each mind.

Then send to us
Your saving grace
When we bow
Each tear-soaked face.

We ask of You,
Your forgiving love
To wash down on us
From up above.

Lord, Cover Me

I'm worn down,
So worn down,
Lord, cover me
With Your golden crown.

I've lost my way,
Lord, lost my way,
Come lift me up
From the miry clay.

I cannot see,
I'm blind to see,
Lord, blow Your breath
And set me free.

I feel His pain,
Jesus' racking pain,
Lord cover me
With healing rain.

I walk alone,
Feel so alone,
Lord cover me
And take me home.

The empty tomb
And the rugged cross,
I share with You, Lord,
Your heartfelt loss.

I want to pray,
I bow to pray,
Lord, cover me
With grace today.

Oh, joyful song
That I will sing –
Your sweet grace,
You lovingly bring.

The Proof of Care

In my despair,
I bow in prayer
Unable to give
My life half-lived.

In remorseful grief
I seek relief,
Healing again
From anguish and pain.

In this prayer room,
I bow in gloom,
Behind closed door,
I plead once more.

With words that falter
Down at Your alter,
I ask in love
For peace from above.

Keep me today
And strengthen, I pray,
In this turbulent time,
Feed this hungry mind.

So I might be free,
I speak out to Thee
To offer up prayer
As proof that I care.

Walking Beside Us

Oh, that we should come in prayer
More often than we do
And in humble reverence
Lift our needs to you.

Tell You that we're thankful
For Your precious Son
Who died on Calvary's tree
So victory could be won.

Come in joyful praises
Lifting voices high,
Waving our glory banners
Proudly in the sky.

Oh, that we should travel
Down the path of life
And be prepared to tackle
Any negative strife.

For You walk beside us
And never pass us by
Then in the cruelest moments,
You comfort when we cry.

Now we bow in happiness,
Joy written on each face
And thank You, Lord, for giving us
Your amazing grace.

Progression of Christ

I see the star
In dark of night
Shine on a stable
With brilliant light.

I see the water
And descending dove
That bathed this Man
In waves of love.

I see the struggle
Waged all alone
With no thought of fortune
Or golden throne.

I see the miracle
When donkey trod
Into that city
With the Son of God.

I see the love
God has for me
And why His Son
Died on the tree.

I see the pain
In those sad eyes
As on the cross,
He began to cry.

I see the tomb –
He is not there
As grave clothes lay
Unused and bare.

And last of all,
I feel the wind
And know full well,
God did send Him.

A Redemptive Request

Heavenly Father,
We bow at Your mercy seat
Lifting voices of thanksgiving
For Your redemptive love.
Hear our prayers of concern
For the sick and malnourished,
Strengthen the weak
And feed those who hunger.
Comfort those who mourn
And are displaced by conflict and war.
Purge the iniquity of this world, Lord,
And continue to lead us
In the path of righteousness
For Your name's sake.

Amen

Women of the Bible

Women of the bible,
We can all tell,
Are instruments of God
And He has used them well.

From Old Testament times
Up until today,
Women of the bible
Had their story to say.

Washed by His blood,
They worked for God,
No matter the service
Or country they trod.

Filled by God's Spirit,
Women so bold,
Stepped out in faith,
So we are told.

Led men into battle
And others in song,
Humble they grew,
Doing no wrong.

Whether in the forefront
Or in the background,
Women of the bible –
Their faith grew strong.

Women of the bible,
Do not forget them
For how they loved God
And served only Him.

Precious Moments

Lord, we are so humbled
By how You watch over us
For in the hours of darkness,
You do not groan or fuss.

We hoard the precious moments
That with You we share
For in those days of sorrow,
Life is easier to bear.

This load we could not carry
If alone we walk
So leaning on the promise,
We listen to You talk.

We drink Your living waters,
At Your table, we all sup
So thank You, Lord, for filling
Each and every cup.

It is those precious moments
When our faith You renew,
Searching for Your kindness
As we come to You.

Joy of Thanksgiving

Reflect in October,
Our glad hearts sing,
The joy of Thanksgiving
This month can bring.

Turkey and dressing,
Vegetables and pie,
Thanksgiving we give
To You on high.

Remind us once more
Of the riches we sing,
Showered from heaven
By our coming King.

Thank You, Lord Jesus,
For all that we see
And for the blessings
Poured out by Thee.

Passage of Time

How reckless we are
With time on our hands,
Never a thought
Of that humble Man.

Never a glimpse
In the bible to see
The wonderful stories
And how they could be.

Never a question
Of why He loves us,
No, not a thought
Just too busy to fuss.

But when life goes wrong,
Our hearts full of pain,
We reach out to God
For His healing rain.

Why did we wait
And pass Him by
Till all of a sudden,
We think we might die?

Well, there is a time,
Now you feel sad,
That God will forgive us –
Forget all the bad.

Now there is time
For you and me
To call out in prayer,
Having God set us free.

Eternal Love

Sadly weeps
This heart of mine
With mournful voice,
I soulfully pine.

Lord, lift me up
When I'm cast down,
Remove from me
This deepening frown.

Purge the pain
From my broken heart,
Fill me with grace
For a new start.

So I can sing
The songs of praise
And clap my hands,
Your joy I raise.

I will play
The harp and lyre
As in my heart
Grows the burning fire.

Because Your grace
Comes from above,
I'll sing the hymn
Of eternal love.

Loving Faith

Father God,
We offer up thanksgiving
For answered prayer.
Thank You, Lord,
For filling our needs
When we ask in loving faith.
Continue to pour
Your grace and blessings
Out upon those
Who are unable

To ask for themselves.
Lord, we know Your love
And spiritual grace
Surpasses all understanding
And we ask in the name
Of Jesus Christ
That Your love and glory
Spreads and flourishes
In every hungry heart
Around the world today.

Amen

God's Promise

You know our joy
And feel our pain,
By Your wisdom,
Your grace we gain.

Through dark valleys,
We walk with You
And on mountaintops,
You go with us, too.

We conquer life
With You at our side,
Our joy for Your love,
We cannot hide.

We have the promise
That every day,
Right there beside us,
You will stay.

During the darkness,
You light our way,
So in thanksgiving,
We humbly pray.

When battles are fought
And each victory's won,
We thank You, Lord,
For Your precious Son.

Small Stuff

Don't sweat the small stuff,
For it is true,
God is right here
To take care of you.

Remember the raven –
He stores no food
So God will look after
All that is good.

Don't try to dissect
What people say,
Step out in faith
With our Saviour today.

Don't sweat the small stuff,
God makes it known,
He tends all his crops,
Fertile seed He has sown.

We are His harvest
And nothing comes cheap,
Because of sweet Jesus,
Our love He will reap.

Don't sweat the small stuff,
Grow straight and tall
For leaning on Jesus
Makes life worth it all.

The Ransom

The ransom price
That Jesus gave,
He made for all
Who might be saved.

This price so high
We understand
On that day of passion,
He's no ordinary Man.

So we should give,
Through love and prayer,
To our fellow man
And show we care.

There is no gift
That can be compared
To our Saviour
And how He shared.

The scripture fulfilled,
The ransom paid
By God's only Son
And the difference He made.

Preventative Measures

He paid the price
On Calvary's tree
When Jesus died
For a wretch like me.

Now I bow down
In grateful prayer
To thank You, Lord,
For being there.

How do we measure
This amount of love
That came from God's
Heavenly throne above.

For ordinary man
In this modern day,
There's no price too large
For us to repay.

No mountain's too high,
No river's too deep
Which prevents us today
God's love to keep.

Come spread God's word
To all of mankind –
Be disciples today
To the lost and the blind.

A New Beginning

Death is the beginning
Of a new life for me,
I'll wander the clouds
To be happy and free.

I'll sing the old hymns
And gospel songs,
We heard as children
Telling right from wrong.

I'll travel the byways
Up in the sky
To talk with the saints
Waiting on high.

I'll see mountaintops
And rainbows each day,
Then shake people's hands
I meet on the way.

I'll drink from the river
Of Life as it flows
I want to see heaven
And the colours it shows.

I would like to go
Where our Saviour reigns
And know that forever
There is no more pain.

It's just the beginning
A new life I see
That's free for the asking
For you and for me.

The Ultimate Price

In a blink of an eye,
He passed this way –
I scarcely could hear
What He had to say.

When He was gone
And out of sight,
Those loving words
Shone pure as light.

Why didn't I listen
When He passed by?
Lord, hear this lament
As I sadly cry.

Come back this way,
Remove my hate,
Purge one more heart
Before it's too late.

Lord, return this way,
Oh, tell us why
On lonely cross,
You had to die.

The ultimate price
You had to pay
Because we never listened
When You passed this way.

The Empty Cross

Oh, sting of death,
You've crossed our way
With broken hearts,
We mourn today.

In dark of night,
You had your way,
At the graveside,
We bow to pray.

The cross is empty
That bore God's Son,
Oh, sting of death,
Your work is done.

You hear our voices,
Our cries of pain,
Oh, sting of death,
What did you gain?

The promise was written
For us all
But sting of death,
It was your call.

Oh, sting of death,
Now go your way
And leave us alone
To grieve and pray.

Infinite Grace

We pray for neighbours
Who are sick and in pain –
In Your infinite grace,
You send healing rain.

We needn't list their ailments
For You already know
By Your infinite grace,
Our prayers will show.

Lord, our prayer list
Grows longer every day,
At Your mercy seat,
We take time to pray.

That reassuring comfort
You pour out today,
Answers every question
That we send Your way.

With our humble voices,
We praise Your holy Name
And in gratefulness we stay
Faithfully the same.

Amen

For It Is I

Jesus wept,
His love I see
Hanging alone
On Calvary's tree.

Do not weep,
My Lord, for me,
For it is I
Who cries for Thee.

It is I
Who cries real tears –
How You removed
My inner fears.

For it is I
Whose heart is torn
At sight of whip
And crown of thorns.

For it is I
Who cast the stone
And refused to go
With you in scorn.

Now it is I
Who kneels in prayer
At empty tomb –
For You're not there.

And it is I
Beneath the tree
Who feels Your breath
Flow over me.

Lord, let me weep
A tear for You
To prove my love
Is loyal and true.

Lord, let me lift
My tear-soaked face
To thank You for
Your saving grace.

Heavenly Home

I cry, I cry
Out to my God,
Forgive this sinner,
Don't spare the rod.

This heart is broken –
From heaven above,
Can You, my Lord,
Pour out Your love?

Will You repair
And set things right
As I bow to repent
In dark of night?

In humbleness,
I call to Thee,
Forgive this sinner
And set me free.

So in this place
That I call home,
I bow in prayer
Before Your throne.

For in humility,
I come to pray
And thank You, Father,
For that coming day.

In shining light,
Amid trumpet calls,
We come to live
In hallowed halls.

In Your home
Where freedom reigns,
There's eternal life
Without any pain.

Joy and Love

With joy, we sing
Our song of love
And lift our voices
To God above.

With grateful hearts,
We sing out praise
Thanking Jesus for
His loving ways.

Oh, love divine,
Hear glad hearts sing,
This hymn to You,
We happily bring.

Oh, Majesty,
We repeat this phrase
In humble worship,
Our voices raise.

Lift Your hands,
Oh, glory raise
And sing these words
Of joy and praise.

To You, our Father
In heaven above,
We sing our songs
Of blessed love.

Humility

Heavenly Father,
How we rejoice
In the glory of Your salvation.
Oh, that we be counted worthy
Of Your peace and love.
Impart upon us, Lord,
The need to remain
Constant in prayer
In order to increase
Not only our own faith,
But to intercede
For the welfare of others.
When we falter
And feel trodden down,
It is Your Holy Spirit
That lifts and encourages us
To go forward.
May our works and humility
Be a witness to those
Around us, Lord,
That we not boast
But show forgiveness,
Joy and humbleness
To Your grace and glory,
In Jesus' name, we pray.

Amen

Song of Life

With care we sang
The morning song,
Not sure of where
We all belong.

Then by noon
We sang with joy
And played outside
With a new toy.

Time slips on,
It's growing late,
The song is sad
And tells of hate.

We are bewildered
At words we sing
For there's no joy
This song can bring.

We grow anxious
Over this song
For in our lives,
It doesn't belong.

As nighttime comes
With darkening sky,
This song of life
Makes us cry.

At Day's End

In the dimness
Of dawn's early light,
We thank You, Lord,
For our safe night.

As we bow
Again and pray,
We ask for peace
Throughout the day.

At Your table,
We bow each head
To thank You, Lord,
For broken bread.

At our bedside,
We kneel and say
How grateful we are
At end of day.

Amen

The Lament

In death, we cry
This lament
Of mounting grief
And discontent.

In death, we wail
Our voices sad,
With broken hearts,
We feel so bad.

In death, we see
Beyond the grave –
Why our loved ones
Were so brave.

Because of death,
We learn to pray,
Calling out to God
In a different way.

And in death,
Our voices sing
Asking You, Lord,
To remove the sting.

The pain of death –
We want to be
Released from its hold
And then set free.

Rekindle Faith

From God's holy breath,
The fire burns
And rages in hearts
As lost souls return.

Rekindle your faith
To renew the love
That comes from our Father
In heaven above.

When souls grow parched
And faith dries up,
Drink living waters
From God's cup.

Be prepared
To lose it all
If you ignore
The Spirit's call.

God doesn't forget
Or push you aside,
Come talk to Him –
Don't run and hide.

At day's end,
You can be
Released from fear
And set free.

24 Hours

The night grows black,
I've lost my way
In the struggle of life,
I went astray.
In misty light
Of early dawn,
I cannot see
And stumble on.
In heat of day,
I cry in pain,
Do you hear
This sad refrain?
As twilight beckons
And waves to me,

With lack of faith,
I cannot see.
The minutes tick by,
I've lost my way,
In those 24 hours
When I could not pray.
The veil is lifted,
I call out to Thee,
Oh, Lord, can You hear
And set me free?
In humble voice,
I bow and say,
"Thank You, Father,
For leading the way."

Proclaim God's Love

Sing out in joy,
Oh, love divine
To cleanse this aching
Heart of mine.

Heal the hurt
That fills this soul,
Lead the way
You want me to go.

I seek release
From any strife
That hinders Your Spirit
In my life.

I come to You
In earnest prayer
Because I know
How much You care.

A promise written
In Your words of love
Showered upon us
From heaven above.

I need Your grace,
Oh, love divine,
To soothe my heart
And troubled mind.

God's Book

There is much to digest
When reading God's word
And how on mankind,
His grace was poured.

We should read with care
And give it much thought
Of why in life,
His love we sought.

Sometimes it's hard
To understand it all,
When searching the gospels,
We can hear God call.

Faith steps in
To clear our minds
So we can remember
The important lines.

Well, that's it!
Now I can see
The wisdom God has
In His word for me.

Through prayer and study
We can now hear
How God has helped
To remove our fear.

Help the Suffering

Lord, we pray for those
Who struggle to live,
We ask for Your shelter
And goodness to give.

We pray for those who've
Lost jobs and homes
That the basics are provided
Like meals and rooms.

We pray for a filling
Of compassionate love
That comes from us
And from God above.

We ask for encouragement
To help those along
So they may have comfort
When everything's gone.

Lead us to turn
Our differences aside,
To reach out in charity
Not walk away and hide.

Teach us, Lord, to be,
At whatever the cost,
A help to the suffering
And a friend to the lost.

The Kindness of God

The blood that flowed
At Calvary's tree,
Will purge our hearts
And set us free.

The broken bread
And wine-filled cup,
Help us remember
When coming to sup.

The love of Christ –
He was so kind
To sinner and leper
And to the blind.

Not one ignored
No woman or man,
No beggar or child
Throughout the land.

For common folk,
He came their way
And warned kings
Not to go astray.

With patience and love,
He gathered with him,
Twelve disciples
To be fishers of men.

Then one sad day,
Christ was gone
To His heavenly Father
Where He belonged.

So here on earth,
We can sing a song –
God gave His Son
To right all wrong.

Blessings and Grace

How we are blessed
By God's grace,
It is the triumph
Of life's race.

By our faith
In giving all,
We are blessed
For it is God's call.

Blessings and grace
Go hand in hand
And are freely given
To every man.

What more could
We ask or expect?
Blessings and grace
Make life perfect.

Paid for by Jesus
On the tree,
Blessings and grace
Are for you and me.

So humble yourself
Before God's throne,
For blessings and grace
Will take us all home.

Encouragement and Joy

Through valleys deep,
We walk alone,
Too proud to come
To Your throne.

But in a season
Of being sad,
We pray to You
For the joy we had.

Lord, hear our cries
As we call in pain,
Answer our plea
Just once again.

And in our distress,
We will sing in prayer,
An honest thanksgiving
For hearing us there.

Knowing full well
That You fill us up
As we drink every drop
That pours from Your cup.

Thank You for answering
Our earnest prayer,
For the encouragement
That proves You care.

The Light

The light grew dim
In the dark,
What good is this
Faint little spark?

Over the years,
That light, it grew,
And far away,
You could see it, too.

The light became
A joyful flame
And it was said
To remove the shame.

Then in time,
That searing light
Lit up the world
In dark of night.

So people gathered
To dance and sing
In this light,
Much joy they bring,

The light was battered
Then tossed about
And we were afraid
It would go out.

On Calvary's tree,
That light grew dim
From the insult
That happened to Him.

In our hearts,
A spark grows bright
This flame shines out
To light the night.

Heart's Door

How lucky I am,
A rich person, I cry,
For I have met Jesus
And know why He died.

I walked the deep valley
In dark of the night
But never to fear
Guided by Jesus' light.

Oh, what a promise
For this changing start
Because Jesus has filled
All of my heart.

Sing out in joy,
Talk to Jesus today,
Open your heart's door –
He's walking this way.

Reach out to Jesus,
Don't run and hide,
Open your heart's door –
He'll step inside.

No hesitation,
Don't stumble and fall,
Reach out to Jesus
And answer God's call.

Joy and Praise

Heavenly Father,
Remove any uncertainty
From our minds
And renew a right spirit
Within our hearts.
Teach us, Lord, to be happy
In our prayer life,
Coming to Your throne of grace
With songs of adoration and praise.

Fill us with joy and peace, Father,
That people see and understand
That praise and prayer go together.

In our search for healing and comfort,
We honour Your glory
With praise and thanksgiving.
In Jesus name, we pray.

Amen

A Moment Lost

Lord, is there a task
I did not do
Or a prayer
Not sent to You?

Was there a judgment
Which I passed
That's uncalled for
And should not last?

Did I forget
My fellow man
Because of pride
Didn't shake his hand?

Did I fail to come
And kneel to pray
Forgetting the needs
Of others today?

Was there a chance
I did not take
To thank Your Son
For His Name's sake?

Was there a cry
I did not hear,
A chance passed by
To calm a fear?

Was there a moment
I did not say,
"Thank You, Father,
For today?"

Prayer of Blessing

Heavenly, Father,
We are humbled by Your
Abiding mercy and love.
Thank You for the many blessings
Showered upon us
That we often take for granted.
Lord, thank You,
For the presence of Your Holy Spirit,
And for Your strength and comfort
That each day brings.
Continue to pour Your grace
And blessings on those
Less fortunate than ourselves.
We will be careful
To give You all honour,
Glory and praise.
In Jesus' Name.

Amen

Harvest Grace

Heavenly, Father,
We thank You
For this harvest feast,
May Your grace
Continue to nourish
Body and soul
And may our friendship
Be pleasing in Your sight.
And together,
Your people say –

Amen

Healing Souls

With Loving Hearts
We come to pray
For lost souls
Along life's way.

The burdens they bear,
We know not why,
Their hearts are broken
And they cry.

Sad stories they tell
Of years gone by,
The battles they fought
And of friends that die.

Together we bow
And ask of Thee,
To heal these souls
And set them free.

Free to fly
On golden wings,
Free from the worries
That death brings.

Fly on the clouds
In angels' light,
To steal the dread
Of life's dark night.

We bow and pray
To ask and sing,
Healing for these souls
That You bring.

A Holy Visit

Wait! Oh, wait!
Don't run away –
Come bow your head
With me to pray.

Let's visit with God,
He's like an old Friend,
Come with me,
Your voice to lend.

God loves to listen,
Do not fear,
Come speak softly
In His Ear.

He will not leave
Or walk away,
Come talk to God
And have your say.

Come visit with God,
He really does care,
Speak out in faith,
He'll answer your prayer.

Don't be shy,
Come bow your face
And feel the warmth
Of His saving grace.

He will not leave you
Here alone,
Now trust in God
To guide you home.

When Minutes Tick By

May God comfort and bless you
In your journey alone,
Remember God heals
From His heavenly throne.

When minutes tick by
In your season of grief,
Feel how He loves you
And offers relief.

We pray for help
And encouragement, too,
Reach out to the Father
To carry you through.

May comfort and strength
From God's loving grace
Be part of the healing
In all that you face.

What More Can There Be?

In Reverence, we enter
The throne room of God
To offer thanksgiving
For life's road that we trod.

All glory and honour,
We sing onto Thee,
Oh, gracious wonder,
What more can there be?

Now in humbleness,
We pray joyfully,
To thank You, dear Father,
For Calvary's tree.

Renew us with vigour,
Throw open the doors
As our songs of glory
Dance over the floors.

Go into the world
To tell all that we see
Of God's saving grace,
What more could there be?

Because of Jesus

It is God's love
We don't deserve
When we forget
And rattle His nerves.

It is our faith
That takes a dive
When secular treasures
Make us slide.

It is God's plan
For eternal life,
That we seek
An end to strife.

Was it not enough
That He gave His Son
So we'd claim victory
For battles won?

At God's mercy seat,
Let us ask once more
For His forgiveness
To settle the score.

We should sing out
And tell our Lord
Because of Jesus,
His name is adored.

Nurturing Prayer

Heavenly Father,
We thank You
For the power of the cross
And the presence
Of Your Holy Spirit.
We thank You
For the working of Your grace
In our lives.
Father, continue to nurture us
Through Your word
And sustain us
In every peril
That we face.
Lord, continue to remove
The temptations from our lives
And walk closer
With Your people
Along our journey with You.
In Jesus' name, we pray.

Amen

Serving God

Lord, if there is a season of doubt
Or discontent in our lives,
Lead us through Your word.
Guide us into deeper prayer
And meditation.
Draw us closer to Your grace
That we have a clear understanding
Of Your intention
For our service to You.
Give us joyful voices
And Thankful hearts.
Lord, give Your people
A spirit of love
To help those less fortunate
Than ourselves
And to remain vigilant in prayer.
In Jesus' name, we ask.

Amen

The Crowds

See the crowds gather
In Jesus' sight,
Searching for knowledge
Of God's light.

See the crowds gather
Just to be fed
Manna from heaven
With fishes and bread.

See the crowds gather
Waving palm branches high
As into the city,
Jesus rides by.

See the crowds gather
Beyond all belief
To cry for His death
Just to save a thief.

See the crowds gather
There at the cross
When all of a sudden
They realize their loss.

See the crowds search
Over the years
For God's compassion
That pours out like tears.

Rescued

On the bumpy road
Of my life,
I struggled through
Hardship and strife.

Walking alone,
The tears would flow
In time of trouble,
It worried me so.

Then I met a fellow
Who rescued me,
He said He came
From Galilee.

Take outstretched hand
And pray with me,
You'll not walk alone –
I will travel with thee.

Such comforting words,
My heart they filled,
Then into my soul,
His Spirit spilled.

The road is still bumpy –
The walk's a delight
For I'm not alone
Travelling in God's sight.

Holy Music

The ministry of music –
Don't count it out
Sing to the Lord,
And give a shout.

Lift voices of praise,
Hear organs play
These hymns of glory,
We sing today.

Sing songs of triumph
As trumpets blow,
Sing out to God
Songs we love so.

See smiles on the faces
As small children sing
Beloved choruses,
Their voices ring.

Sing glory verses
As music is played –
Words tell the story
That we live this way.

Come sing the music
That sets hearts on fire
Played by the organ,
The harp and the lyre.

Life's Road

I had not walked
This road before
As God's love,
I did not know.

I had not bowed
My head in prayer
For no one said
That God does care.

But one stormy
And black night,
I met the Lord
In death's fright.

A child was taken
From this earth,
I had never felt
So much hurt.

On bedroom floor,
I cried out in pain
And soon God sent
His comforting rain.

I felt the warmth
Of God's breath
As He whispered gently
Of my child's death.

Now I walk
Through sun and rain,
The road no longer
Holds death's pain.

For I have found
God walking there
And now life's road
Holds no despair.

Sad Voices

At the gravestones,
Hear sad voices cry,
Try hard not to linger
Where our dear children lie.

Our prayers ring out
From hearts full of pain,
Listen intently
To this sad refrain.

For a moment of comfort,
Now give us some ease
As we pray out to God
Down here on our knees.

There at the gravestones,
Where the poppies all cry,
What causes life's battles
That make children die?

Questions need answers,
We ask day and night,
Will Your holy angels
Shine on us some light?

Sad voices cry out,
Don't linger here,
For only God's comfort
Will dry up our tears.

Sharing the Load

Heavenly Father,
Continue to shine
Your light upon us
When we struggle in the dark.
When the load of life
Becomes unbearable,
We hold to the promise
That You will share this weight
That burdens us.
Remove any obstacle
That blocks the vision
You hold for us and teach us, Lord,
To be ever mindful of the blessings
And grace You pour out
Upon Your humble servants.
In Jesus' name, we pray.

Amen

God's Way

We struggle for comfort
In a season of grief
And because of Your Son
Are filled with relief.

You see broken hearts
And spirits grown numb,
It is in this hour
To You that we come.

Oh, for Your love,
A release from our pain,
Only from You, Lord,
Such strength we do gain.

You gave Your Son
That we might live
To You comes all glory –
What else can we give?

We'll make the time
Before it's too late
To bow down in prayer
At Your open gate.

Offer our voices
In thanksgiving today
Because of sweet Jesus
He's shown us the way.

Wonder of Life

From snowflakes to raindrops,
The wind that blows free
And for the birds
That nest in the tree.

To small busy bees
And the honey they make,
Healthy and sweet
In the goodies we bake.

Sunbeams and rainbows,
Clouds in the sky,
Are the wonder of life
From birth till we die.

That gift of spring
When grass turns green
With small flower buds
Answers a dream.

The brilliance of fall
As leaves tumble down,
A touch of white frost
That looks like a crown.

The Master created it
For us to live in,
Then down on our knees
We can thank Him.

In songs of thanksgiving,
Lift voices of praise
For all God has provided
Our joyful hearts raise.

This wonder of life,
We're so rich and blessed,
So offer God glory
In words we confess.

The Stable

Across the sand
Three camels came
Ridden by wise men
Of wealth and fame.

Going to Bethlehem
With spices and gold,
Travelling through darkness
Guided by starlight bold.

Into the stable
Where the baby lay
With cattle and sheep
There on the hay.

Then came the shepherds,
So humble and meek
Into this place,
The Saviour they seek.

A night of emotion,
The world, it stood still,
For God's holy promise
Could this baby fulfill.

In quiet reverence,
They humbly pray
For God's only Son
Born on Christmas day.

God's Invitation

You won't find me
In the phone book
Because I'm next to you.
You might think I
Stay with rich folk
But I love the ailing
And the blue.
Don't look for me
In newspapers,
I'm hardly ever there.
So if you want to visit,
Just bow your head in prayer.
If you need a guide book,
I'll tell you what to use –
It's the holy bible,
Read of the good news.
Don't worry about the direction
You think you should go
For I walk beside you
And I already know.
Don't visit just when lonely
Or in desperate need,
Come show your appreciation
For the bread
On which you feed.
Come visit anytime,
My door is open wide,
Do not be afraid –
Feel free to step inside.

A Prayer of Service

Heavenly Father, forgive us
As we bow in prayer.
Close our ears and minds
To idle gossip, so we are
Not tempted to repeat
Things that may damage
Reputations or friendships.
Thank You, Lord,
For giving us a more important
Task to complete in service
To our fellow man.
Lord, thank You
For comforting words and encouragement
And for opening our minds
To the wisdom of Your word.
Continue to teach us
The need for Christian charity
And mission in our community,
Our country and around the world today.
Teach us to give with loving hearts
Expecting no praise or recognition in return.
Father, continue to keep us
Humble in thought and work
So our service to You remains constant
And pleasing in Your sight.
In Jesus' Name, we pray.

Amen

Believe in Jesus

Down in the stable,
Hear angels sing,
It is good news
That they bring.

The birth of a child,
In writing is told,
One night in Bethlehem,
Dark and cold.

To Mary and Joseph,
God promised all,
A Son would be born
To answer God's call.

A Saviour and King
To walk across land,
Forthright and humble
Come hear this man.

Hear what he says,
See His healing touch,
Meet the disciples
Who love Him so much.

Follow the footsteps
Across the burning sand,
Listen to the parables
Taught by this Man.

Hear the words spoken,
Be sure to take heed
For this humble Saviour
Is planting God's seed.

See wooden tree
Where He will cry
For you and me,
Our Saviour shall die.

But love is not lost,
God says to us all,
Believe in this Jesus
And answer His call.

Nothing Was New

A building made of logs
With a thick wooden door,
A firm foundation
Holding up the floor.

Second hand pews –
The pulpit was, too.
Even the hymn books,
For nothing was new.

A heavy steel stove
Blasted out heat,
Wood snapping and cracking,
Now don't fall asleep.

Here is God's presence,
So warm and so real,
Touching bowed heads,
You could just feel.

The pastor's voice travelled,
Smooth and so slow
Through bible verses
You came to know.

A half dozen farmers
With thinning white hair,
Bowed their heads
In comforting prayer.

No, nothing was new
In this building so dim,
Only His presence
And spiritual hymn.

Fruits of Your Labour

It's the people you meet
Along life's way
That encourage you greatly
In their own way.

Humble and meek,
Such love and grace,
You realize it comes
From a higher place.

When you think back
On things they said,
Much of that wisdom
In God's word you read.

When you meet a person
Troubled and in pain,
Pray with him lovingly
In Jesus' Name.

A word softly spoken,
A squeeze of the hand,
Does much to lift up
A disheartened man.

The fruits of your labour
Will multiply, too,
When you help another
Who's feeling so blue.

My Comforting Friend

I'd be upset
If we weren't friends,
Your sense of humour
Has no end.

Those comforting things
You often say
That little hug
When I have a bad day.

You're always home
Whenever I call,
You're there to listen
When I slip and fall.

The coffee pot's on,
A chair is pulled out
At Your kitchen table
When I come about.

I really do wonder
If you think like me –
You're always prepared
When I come to see.

With bible in hand
And head bowed low,
The questions I ask,
You already know.

Whenever I'm sad
And cry a tear,
You reassure me
And calm every fear.

So, Lord, I pray
Our friendship stays strong
Forever and ever
Until time is gone.

December 24

Father God,
Thank You for
The miraculous birth
Of Your precious Son.
May all mankind
Celebrate this true
And joyous event
That is Christmas.
Lord, keep us ever mindful
Of the Babe in the manger
That we celebrate
The humble birth
That the wise men
And shepherds witnessed
In its simple glory.
Lord, may we all understand
This very beginning
Of Your Son's glorious reign
As King and Saviour.
We reflect and are humbled
By His majesty
And the working
Of the Holy Spirit
In our lives today.
To You, be all praises,
Honour and glory.

Amen

Reviving Faith

A sinner I am,
A wretch I will be,
Hear me, oh, Father
As I cry out to Thee.

In my search for Your grace,
Wash me anew,
When bowing in shame,
I call out to You.

Through Jesus' blood
Spilt on Calvary's tree,
I see what you've done
For sinners like me.

At Your mercy seat,
Have Your own way –
When this sinner
Bows down to pray.

Asking forgiveness,
Pour out onto me,
Love and compassion
Your gift that is free.

Purge me and cleanse me
Reviving my faith
As I ask for a filling
Of Your saving grace.

Amen

A Rescued Sinner

When a sinner is rescued
By God's own love,
We see the spiritual power
That comes from above.

We are amazed
Oh, Father divine,
Another branch is added
To Your living vine.

The fruit of Your labour
Won't fall from the tree
But is picked by angels
To be used by Thee.

To Ripen and mellow
Like the new wine
For You, precious Father,
Take Your own time.

Don't hurry around,
To rush the process
You handle so gently,
We must confess.

When a sinner is rescued,
We watch with delight
At the change that is rendered
In Your comforting sight.

The Pain of Judas

Lord, do not dry
The wretched tears
On this traitor's face,
For it is I
Who took the coins
And brought the soldiers
To that place.

In loathing, I tremble
For what I've done,
The greed of silver
No victory is won,
I cannot bear
Those eyes of love,
His look of compassion
That came from above.

Take me from here
And let me die
For this terrible deed
When an innocent will cry.

The judgment is Yours,
Not worthy am I,
To walk this path
Where Jesus will die.
Lord, take me from here,
Let me breathe my last breath
For pointing My Saviour
To His suffering and death.

Modern Day Marys

They are the Marys
Who go on once more,
All the brave mothers
Who lost sons in war.

The crosses they bear
In each broken heart
From their brave sons
So peace could start.

Modern day Marys,
Hearts open and sore,
How heavy the pain is,
That they all bore.

The grief on their faces
Now says it all –
The price of our peace
Paid by freedom's call.

Modern day Marys
Don't settle the score,
They bow at the cross
All praying once more.

Modern day Marys,
A new price is paid
By the young sons
Who lie in their graves.

Steal Away, Too

When we weren't looking
God took You home,
From the pathway
And trail that we roam.

Yes, our hearts were broken
And we shed a tear
But we accepted
That God has drawn near.

From the gardens of this world,
He lifted you on high
To walk on golden pathways
Up there In the sky.

No longer filled
With racking pain,
Now we can hear
You laughing again.

God in His wisdom
And mercy divine,
Has put You in
A new place sublime.

There patiently waiting
For that crowning day
When we shall gather
And come Your way.

The Pilgrimage

The pilgrimage lasted
For days on end,
This road carefully taken
With its sharp bend.

Travelled through towns
And villages, too,
Hosted by strangers
They never knew.

Onward they trekked,
The group grew in size,
Into the unknown
To claim their prize.

Barefooted and tired,
The road appeared long
But day after day,
Their spirits grew strong.

What lay ahead
For all to encounter?
Did they go in fear
As onward they wandered?

This pilgrimage lasted,
Embarked on by men,
Stout-hearted and weary,
No anger in them.

Then into view,
A town did appear,
With towers and chapels
And bells ringing clear.

Brave men on their knees,
See how they all care,
Complaisant and humble
In silent prayer.

The pilgrimage over
This sacred place reached
By a band of men
Who have come to preach.

Do Not Be Afraid

A scriptural message
We may hold dear
From God's holy word,
We can now hear.

Spoken to those
Who witnessed His glory
By angels and prophets
It's told in the story.

Wise men and shepherds,
The despised and meek,
Those who are sick
And hearts of the weak.

Then to the children
Who sat on His knee,
We hear words spoken
So gently by Thee.

"Do not be afraid,
You have nothing to fear,"
Whispered Jesus,
"Now don't shed a tear."

Written to all,
Sung in cherished hymns,
Do not be afraid
To come unto Him.

When they are spoken
Or read from the psalms,
Feel God's loving Spirit
Like encompassing arms.

Transformation

On life's journey,
I can plainly see
The transformation
God is making in me.
From famine to feast,
Come drink and eat
His bread of life
That is so sweet.
Rejoice in the presence
Of a Spirit divine
Who transforms us all
Like the new wine.
Whenever we stumble
Down the wrong path,
Jesus delivers us
From the devil's wrath.

When in darkness,
We lose our sight,
It is our Saviour
Who shines so bright.
Pointing and guiding us
In the right way,
He gives us the strength
To face each day.
On humble knees,
Come bow down in prayer
And thank Him for showing
He really does care.
Rejoice and sing out
Our songs of love,
Come praise our Saviour
On His throne above.

Bow in God's Presence

Heavenly Father,
Strengthen this weary
Heart of mine
As I bow in Your presence
That is divine.
Wash me and cleanse me,
This soul to renew
With a clear understanding
Of my love for You.

Purge me with spices,
Your hyssop and myrrh,
Remove the bad feelings
That make life a blur.

Fill this empty cup
As I lift it to Thee,
Come change these feelings
That wash over me.
Renew Your right Spirit
In this hungry soul,
Come fill me and feed me
So I will be whole.

Give me the grace
To bow before Thee
And raise prayers
Of thanksgiving
For how You bless me.

Amen

Dark Shadows

We walk through dark shadows
And cry a real tear –
For to live without God
Is to suffer in fear.

When we grow old
And experience pain –
To live without God,
We have nothing to gain.

In the dark shadows
Where all life is dim,
How lonely we are
With no light from Him.

The shadows surround us
And take all that we gave –
Without our Lord Jesus,
There's nothing to save.

The shadows o'ertake us,
How we feel sad –
Without the Lord's Spirit,
All life has turned bad.

Creeping into the shadows –
A glimmer of light
And when Jesus comes in,
Dark has turned bright.

The light becomes warmth,
There's no chill in the air,
When God's Spirit descends,
It radiates everywhere.

Spiritual Restoration

In this modern day
Of turbulent fears,
Your feathers cover us
And dry our tears.

Through feast and famine,
We draw from You,
Strength and wisdom
To carry us through.

You fill us with grace
Though we hunger for more,
Searching and asking
Your love to restore.

Your light shines in darkness,
You show us the way
And walk beside us
Through the miry clay.

We call upon You
And Your Spirit divine
We thank You for caring
In our troubled time.

When day is over
And we bow in prayer,
Praises and thanksgiving,
To You we share.

Reservations

It's never too late
To call the Lord
For your reservation
To enter heaven's door.

Call for your ticket –
Do not delay
For God will be coming
To take us away.

Prepare for the flight,
It is easy to do,
Just tell Him you believe,
Ask that He forgive You.

Spill out your troubles,
He hears what You say,
Be honest to the Lord,
Just don't delay.

But I must warn you,
This ticket you get,
It is one way –
So don't you forget.

The riches God offers
In this place we go
Passes all understanding,
More than we know.

New Year's Prayer

Heavenly Father,
We ask that Your grace
Be poured upon us
Throughout this year.
Control our thoughts
And secular needs that we don't stray
From Your plan for us.
We pray for continued health,
For Your direction in our decisions
And our commitment to the work
Of Your church.
May our prayers always
Include the safety and sanctity
Of all Your people
Around the world.
Teach us to be unselfish
And considerate of others.
Give Your people patience
And wisdom as we search
For peace among nations
As well as in our own hearts.
Lord, continue to fill us
With the joy of Your Spirit
As we offer up prayers
Of praise and thanksgiving.
May our thoughts and conversations
Remain pleasing in Your sight.
We ask in Jesus' name.

Amen

In Search of Christ

Each day I looked
In every town
Searching for Christ,
I wandered around.

Learned men, I asked
And wondered why
This Man, Jesus,
Really had to die.

The answers given,
I shunned to hear,
For to my eye,
They brought a tear.

"Could things be different?"
I cried aloud,
"Oh, what happened
Above the cloud?"

This price He paid
To settle the score,
Why did it have to be
So much more?

What was the plan,
The reason why,
That mortal men
Caused Him to die?

All this time,
I looked above
And did not see
God's atoning love.

Then one day,
In prayer of fear,
The answer came
And was so clear.

For now I see
What God did give,
Jesus freed me of sin
That I might live.

Mercy and Grace

Merciful and loving God,
We seek the righteousness
Of Your grace.
Continue to fill our hearts
With Your peace and joy.
Keep us forever mindful
Of Christ's spilt blood at Calvary.
Be merciful, Lord,
To our unintentional sin
And shortcomings.
Lead us through Your holy word
Giving to us a clear understanding
Of Your grace and glory.
Continue to draw us
To Your throne of prayer
Where, in all humbleness
And sincerity,
We seek the forgiveness of sin
And the continued infilling
Of Your Holy Spirit.
In so doing, we lift voices
Of praise and joyfulness,
Thanking You always
For Your Son, Jesus Christ,
Who, in His name, we pray.

Amen

A Heavenly Choir

We see God's glory
Shining on high,
How it lights up
The evening sky.

And when you listen,
Hear the angels sing,
Sweet voices echo
And gently ring.

Our tears dry up
And drift away
For our Lord Jesus
Is coming today.

Sing with trumpet,
Harp and lyre,
Come join in song,
This heavenly choir.

Sing out, sing out,
Oh, do not fear
As His Majesty
Is drawing near.

Rejoice, rejoice,
Sing thankful songs
As Jesus' footsteps
Dance quickly along.

Oh, gentle Saviour,
Can You hear
This heavenly choir
As we draw near.

Starting a New Day

Lord, give me strength
To do my chores this day
And a cheerful smile
For meeting those
I come in contact with.
Invoke upon me a good disposition
And patience to face each challenge
That might come my way.
But, Lord, most of all,
Give me a loving heart,
Full of thanksgiving
That all I say and do this day
Is to Your grace and glory.
I ask in Jesus' name.

Amen

Who and Why

Where do you run
In your time of need,
Do you seek out the Saviour
Or secular greed?

Who lifts you up
When you stumble and fall,
Who answers your prayer
Whenever you call?

Who walks beside you
Holding your hand,
Then lifts and carries you
Over sinking sand?

Who dries your tears
When sadly you cry
For you've lost a friend –
Why did he die?

Who gives you patience
And freedom from sin,
Who opens the door
And invites you in?

Who purchased our ransom
On Calvary's tree,
Then, in His wisdom
Set us all free?

Who do you seek
When bowing in prayer,
To whom do you confess
You truly care?

El Shaddai

God is all sufficient.
He is our strength
In times of weakness.
God is our comfort
In times of grief.
He is our peace of heart
In loneliness and frustration,
A Friend when no one else cares.
He is our consciousness,
Our life, our sustainer,
Our strength in Whom we can trust,
The answer to our prayers,
The light in our darkness,
Joy in sadness
And Peacemaker in tribulation.
Above all, He pours
His spiritual grace upon us,
Going before us, living within us,
Transforming and transfixing us
In the image of His glory.

Refuge and Joy

You, Lord, are my strength and refuge.
When the trials of life are overwhelming,
It is Your Spirit that comforts me.
In darkness, You light the dim path
And because of You, I know
All turbulence will pass.
Your majesty is my reason to rejoice
With thankfulness and praise.
In You, Lord, I trust and call upon,
Seeking Your grace and healing.
To You, Lord, I humble myself
In gratefulness for the blessings
Of Your precious Son, Jesus Christ.

God's Word

Read the story,
Of God's word –
A plan to live by
Have you heard?

Stay away, I ask,
Now try your best,
Do not succumb
To life's cruel test.

This plan for living
Is set aside,
A choice for all,
Don't run and hide.

The choice is free,
It's up to us
To invite God in –
Don't make a fuss.

Come eat His bread
And drink of His wine,
Walk in God's light
That will brightly shine.

Come partake,
Do not despair
For God is waiting
To gladly share.

Peace and Harmony

Heavenly Father,
Teach us to live in harmony,
To search for peace and bow in prayer.
Guide us to walk Your path
And reach out to show we care.
Forgive us for our shortcomings,
For patience that we lose,
Fill us with Your spiritual grace
From head down to our toes.
Keep us ever mindful
Of the bloodshed at Calvary,
Lord, that we should intercede in prayer,
Asking that this world be set free.
In our search for harmony,
Lead us down the golden way,
That we come to rejoice in thankful song
And seek Your will today.
Oh, that we should linger at Your mercy seat,
Father, hear us when we pray.

Amen

Helping Others Heal

Lord, we hunger for Your compassion
When we see loved ones sick and in pain,
We pray in times of trial
To ask for Your healing rain.

Lord, we see the people around us
And how they pass You by
With no thought to human suffering,
They see no need to try.

Lord, we see the weak and lonely,
The crippled and the maimed,
Teach us to intercede
For the orphan and the lame.

Help us to guide the lost,
The minds so old and frail,
Teach us to bear the cost
For all who struggle and fail.

Where the light grows dim,
We lift this prayer to You
Asking, heavenly Father,
To light this world so cruel.

God's Will

God's will be done
And not our own,
Give in to Him,
Come to His throne.

He purged our sins,
They have been bought,
Now bow to Him,
The battle was fought.

Walk the path
He lights for us,
Have no fear
And do not fuss.

Sad tears are gone,
They are washed away,
Be filled with His grace,
Trust Jesus today.

The battle is won,
No need to fight,
Come walk with God,
Be washed in His light.

Comfort God gives,
Do not frown,
Come to the Master
And wear His crown.

A Call for Mercy

Hopefully crying,
Our tears float to Thee,
Forgive us, dear Father,
We ask fervently.

With prayers so humble,
We voice our song,
In the Lord's house,
Right conquers all wrong.

By God's loving power,
We wait for Thee,
To purify and cleanse us,
Then set us free.

We plead for Your mercy
To be poured from above,
Come holy Spirit,
Fill us with Your love.

With voices of thanks,
Joyously lifting to Thee,
We sing out our song
For being set free.

Thank You, dear Father,
For Jesus' death on the tree,
We now understand,
How great love can be.

What Can a Person Do?

I fall so short of God's expectations,
What can a person do?
When I bow in humble prayer,
Oh, Lord, does it please You?

In weakness, I let the devil
Lead my mind astray
And in one shocking moment,
I have lost my way.

When disaster calls,
I struggle back to You,
Tell me, heavenly Father,
What can a person do?

Through trial and tribulation,
I miss Your alter call,
Is it any wonder
That I slip and fall?

The time goes quickly by,
I dream and act the fool
When suddenly I cry,
What can a person do?

Does Sunday worship count
And the missions I give to,
Then partaking of communion,
Lord, what else should I do?

Oh, Lord! I ask again,
What can a person do?
Help me become inspired
To show my love to You.

Cleft of the Rock

With His loving Hand,
God shelters me
In the cleft of the rock
And its safety.

When life drags me down
And I tremble from harm,
Lord, hide me away
'Neath the cleft of Your Arm.

God's safety, I seek,
On Him I rely,
In the cleft of the Rock,
Time passes by.

I come unto You,
Where I can dwell
And hear the Lord call
To say, "All is well."

Purge me with mercy,
Wash me anew,
So my heart is clean
When I come unto You.

Hide me away
In the cleft of His love
And fill me with joy
That comes from above.

The cleft is shelter,
This cleft is God's grace
And here I seek rest
In His holy place.

Endless Compassion

When the guilt of your transgressions
Leaves you crippled in despair,
Come to the heavenly Father,
Kneel down in humble prayer.

Those words honestly spoken,
Rise to God's mercy seat,
He will not turn aside to leave
You lonely on the street.

In His endless compassion,
By the spirit of His grace,
Jesus suffered willingly
As He took our place.

That day on Calvary's hill,
Jesus died upon the tree,
The sacrifice He made –
It was for you and me.

Songs of glorious praise
With joyful voices ring
To Jesus up above,
Our thankful hearts will sing.

Hand in Hand

With God, we walk
The endless shore
Hand in hand
Forevermore.
Through stormy blast
And dark of night
Then heat of day
And burning light.
We feed upon
God's saving grace
And seek His wisdom
In desolate space.
Never more
Do we walk alone

But stare contentedly
On His throne.
Holy Spirit,
Your endless flame
Lights our path
And heals the lame.
In our prayers
Of humility,
We lift glad voices
To worship Thee,
Then sing aloud –
This joyful band
Thanking You, Jesus,
With hand in hand.

Humility and Faith

On humility and faith,
Which should come first
As we drink living waters
To quench our thirst?

Through faith, we grow humble,
I can see it,
Pondering this question,
I nervously sit.

So does humility
Increase our faith?
When reading God's word,
On this I contemplate.

For bowing in prayer,
So humble we are,
Kneeling before God
Doesn't lower the bar.

For I understand
Humility and faith
Will both increase
When we give them space.

Our faith is assurance
And trust in Thee,
So in believing
More humble we'll be.

Then God Rescues Me

There is no love greater
That I can see,
When I tremble in fear,
Then God rescues me.

There is one condition –
I struggle to be free,
In this time of trouble
When God rescues me.

In that hour of frustration
With no end I can see,
Our God hears me whisper,
Then He rescues me.

Life's road has many detours
The path, I cannot see,
By asking in prayer,
Then God rescues me.

This way is not my own
Whatever there may be
For deep within my heart,
God is calling me.

I have many imperfections
He isn't done, you see
For God is still refining
As He rescues me.

To Share God's Love

Why should we petition
For those who don't care
When there are urgent things
To put into prayer?

Why should we pray
For those waging war,
Shouldn't we hope
Someone settles the score?

Why should we pray
For those committing sin
Or for the street people
Who have no shelter within?

Why do we offer
Our food and some coin
To the drug addict
Stripped to his loin?

Because we're the children
Of our Father God,
Perhaps it was us,
The wrong path we trod.

Now it's up to us
Who must share God's love
For doesn't it come
From our Lord above?

In God's House

In the sanctuary,
Where it is holy,
Come listen to
God's loving story.

Hear the words
Read from His book,
Visit this sanctuary
And have a look.

The music sung
Is just divine
As the choir sings
Those words sublime.

In the sanctuary,
When all is still,
The presence of God
Your soul can fill.

As you bow
With wounded heart,
Be prepared for God's
Healing love to impart.

Now in this very
Holy space,
God's Spirit floods
Every place.

Modern Day Beatitudes

Blessed be the Word
    Of the Lord.

Blessed are those
    Who seek His wisdom and truth.

Blessed are those
    Who give and administer
    To the sick and the poor.

Blessed are those
    Who help feed and clothe
    The weak and the hungry.

Blessed are the parents
    Who raise their children
    In the presence of God.

Blessed are those
    Who struggle to help others
    With no thought of personal fame
    Or gain.

Blessed are those
    Who bow in prayer daily
    Searching for forgiveness
    And the infilling of God's Holy Spirit.

Honesty of Thanksgiving

Lord of all mercy and love,
Thank You for answered prayer
And the many blessings
Showered upon us.
When worries burden the soul
And hope turns into hopelessness,
In You, Lord, we find solace and strength.
Because of Your Son, Jesus Christ,
Burdens truly are lifted at Calvary.
When we offer up prayers
At Your throne of grace,
Putting our trust and faith in You,
Hopelessness turns to joy and thanksgiving.
We see and feel Your glory, Lord,
And are able to feed from the presence
Of Your grace and wisdom,
In Jesus' Name, we pray.

Amen

Nothing to Fear

When you're overwhelmed
And fear rushes in,
Then bow in prayer,
Come talk to Him.

When moments are anxious
In frustration, you cry,
Do not lose hope
And wonder why.

For Jesus is listening,
He is very near,
Come talk to Him,
You have nothing to fear.

Our time here is short,
God points the way,
Yes, He is waiting,
Come, have your say.

Lift voices in joy,
Be of good cheer,
Our God hears your song,
You have nothing to fear.

"Have nothing to fear,"
We hear from above,
Then in that moment,
Fills us with His love.

Heavenly Sunshine

Lord, You see us as we are,
No cover-up will do
For nothing can be hidden
From the sight of You
So as our hearts lay open
Bare for You to see,
It is our urgent desire
That You set us free.
We know the yoke was lifted
From us many years ago
By Your only Son –
How You love us so.

In our honest eagerness,
We yearn to walk with Thee,
To travel down the path of life
In faith and humility.
We are Your humble servants
Searching for continued love
Asking You, heavenly Father
To feed us from above.
Sending Your heavenly sunshine,
Glowing ever bright,
We thank You for the privilege
Of walking in Your light.

Praise and Wonder

Heavenly Father, to You only
Do I confess my sins
And lift my voice
In praises and wonder.
You are my Rock and Fortress,
In Whom I trust and believe.
You, Lord, lead me
Through darkness
And comfort me in sadness.
When I hunger for Your grace,
It is You who feeds me
With the bread of life.
It is Your high tower
I seek in despair
And Your Holy Spirit
I cry out to in time of need.
Praise be to You, Lord,
For hearing and answering
The requests of Your humble servant.
In Jesus' Name, I pray.

Amen

Old Friendships

Don't be embarrassed
When you cry,
It's not every day
A loved one dies.

We feel your pain
When you grieve,
Come lay your head
On a stouter sleeve.

We'll lift a prayer
Just for you
And ask God for strength
When you're so blue.

Come hug a friend,
Comfort we've saved
Just to surround you
Out at the grave.

Comfort and friendship,
Words are hard to say
As we offer you both
On this sad day.

So in the future,
Don't make a fuss,
Remember old friendships
And call upon us.

Then all together
In dimming night
We'll rekindle friendships
In God's precious light.

A Humble Prayer

Heavenly Father, we lift voices in prayer,
Calling out to You in thanksgiving and joy.
In our distress, we come to You and wait
For Your instruction and encouragement.
We kneel in awe at Your majesty and Your grace
And realize how humble and insignificant we are,
But in Your love, You count us equal and important.
Continue to lead us, Lord, and feed us
From the table that is prepared for all mankind.
And we shall, in all humbleness,
Offer up our thanksgiving and joyfulness.
In Jesus' Name, we pray.

Amen

Victory March

Live by the biblical roadmap,
Read it every day,
Follow in its wisdom,
Then take time to pray.

Jesus will sustain you,
Follow down His path,
There He will protect You
From the devil's wrath.

If in weakness you might falter,
Feel you're going astray,
Remember He walks with you,
Each and every day.

There is no love greater
Nothing on this land
That will ever compare
To God's almighty Hand.

So do not ramble blindly
Going Your own way
For Christ is here to guide you
In all you do and say.

Walk this road to freedom,
His light will show the way,
Come join this victory march,
God calls your name today.

Walk to Emmaus

That Emmaus road,
So dusty and bare
With a few palm trees
Growing here and there.

Slowly they walked
Hearts broken and sore,
Two lonely men –
What burdens they bore.

Then along came another
Blinded in despair,
The two didn't recognize
That Jesus was there.

They marveled at the stories,
Along their way,
The wisdom He spoke
Gave them comfort that day.

They invited Him to tarry
Spend more time with them
For the day was late
And light had grown dim.

When Christ broke bread
They saw it was He,
Their sad hearts rejoiced
For the Man of Galilee.

Then showing them scars,
The wound in His side,
There was no reason
For these men to hide.

I tell you this story,
Now do not cry
For God had a plan
Why Jesus must die.

Heavenly Crown

Down in the valley
In the middle of town,
A church bell rings out
Its inviting sound.

Calling to worship
God's precious lambs,
Come sing the hymns
Echoing o'er the land.

Hear scripture read
And a message so bold
Speaking to all –
The young and the old.

An old country church
Its service unchanged,
Calling the flock
In wind and the rain.

In sun boiling hot
And winter so cold,
Come to the service
Where the message is told.

Come hear a story
Of humble men
Preaching and teaching
And healing within.

Down in the valley
In the middle of town
Come to this service
For your heavenly crown.

Living with the Saviour

Feel the love of Jesus
Washing from within
Wells of living waters
Cleansing all your sin.

Feel the Holy Spirit
Floating like a dove
Filling heart and soul
In His presence from above.

See the rugged cross
There on Calvary's hill,
Understand that sacrifice
Truly was God's will.

And the empty tomb
For He isn't there
Because the love of Jesus
Abides in us everywhere.

Offer God your service,
Kneel in humble prayer,
Tell Him all your secrets
He is waiting just to hear.

Feel His holy presence,
Light this way once dim,
Come live with the Saviour
And be a part of Him.

Apathy and Grace

Well, apathetic was
A gentle term
To describe this person
So gloomy and stern.

We do not know
What lies within
To make a heart
So hard in him.

To turn a person
Into stone
With no friends
To call his own.

He sat in church
In an empty pew
Spoken to only
By a few.

But that heart of stone
Would melt away
When children stopped
With words to say.

How a smile
Would light his face
Gone was the apathy
Replaced with grace.

No, we do not know
The sorrow he'll bear
Only that God heals
When he kneels in prayer.

The Love of God

Somewhere in
Your weary mind,
The love of God
Is intertwined.

When hope is gone
And spirits low,
The love of God
Helps minds to grow.

Don't turn your back
And walk away –
The love of God
Fills you today.

The love of God
By His grace
Fills every need
That you will face.

When all is lost
And you cry above
Your request is heard,
Through God's love.

Lift prayers of need
And thanksgiving, too,
For the love of God
Will answer you.

Wealth from Above

My little cottage
Where I rest
Is like that of
A robin's nest.

One small room
With firelight
Where I find warmth
On coldest night.

There stands a table
For my bread
And a shelf
Serves as my bed.

In candlelight,
I bow to pray
At end of every
Working day.

A simple place
Makes life complete
From thankful head
To weary feet.

No grand palace
Do I need
For that shows
A human's greed.

Because my wealth
Comes from above
And is multiplied
In God's love.

Stairway to Prayer

In humble prayer,
I climb each stair
To higher ground
For God is there.

Lift up my praise,
Supplications, too
So in that hour,
I can pray through.

God is the meat
For a hungry soul,
He fills my heart,
That is His goal.

But in His wisdom,
He waits very still
As I ask forgiveness
For my stubborn will.

The stairs are steep
But I climb higher
To ask for mercy
Before I retire.

"Oh, precious Lord,"
I call out in shame,
"Forgive this sinner
For I'm to blame."

Then in a moment,
His love flows in
And I rejoice – filled
With the spirit from Him.

To Pray for Others

Heavenly Father, we bow before You,
Seeking Your grace and love.
We honour Your majesty
With glory and praises,
Asking Lord, for:
Healing for the sick,
Food for the hungry,
Strength for the weak,
Forgiveness for the transgressors
And comfort for the tormented.
Lord, we are humbled
By Your endless compassion
And by the grace You shower
Upon Your children.
Continue to teach us Your ways
And keep us mindful
Of the sacrificial gift made
By Your precious Son, Jesus Christ,
In Whose Name, we pray.

Amen

The Cross Glorified

Oh, cross, cry out!
When Jesus died,
His weight you bore,
Now glorified.
Your wood is stained
And precious be
To all who've sinned,
We look at Thee.
You, who witnessed
Death's cruel sting,
Stand all alone –
No song to sing.
His passion lost,
The battle done

And for Christ,
The victory's won,
But such a cost
For this humble man
Who gave His all
On distant land.
We stand in awe
Then bow at His feet
To seek His grace
At God's mercy seat.
Oh, cross, cry out!
For our Saviour died
That all mankind
Might rest at His side.

Halo

My halo is tarnished,
I hide out of sight
Afraid to go out
Till the darkness of night.

I polish that halo –
The shine, it won't come,
Oh, what a sinner
Is this lowly bum.

Where is the joy
That once filled my heart –
Painfully looking for
A life-giving start?

Halo so tarnished –
I'm heartbroken, too,
Oh, Lord, I am searching
All over for You.

When did I lose You?
What has gone wrong?
Sadly, I sing
The words of this song.

Halo is tarnished,
These tears I cry,
Oh, Lord, forgive me –
I'm ready to die.

Holy Communion

He broke the bread
And blessed the wine,
An eternal gesture
Before our time.

But in this action,
We can see
God's complete love
For you and me.

To give His Son
On Calvary's hill
That we might live
Haunts us still.

Love so true
To lose a Son
That sin be forgiven,
This victory is won.

A humbling moment,
We work to be
More thoughtful and thankful
For how we are set free.

That precious blood
Spilt from Thee
The broken bread
Offered on that tree.

This love of Christ,
So short we fall
Now come to answer
God's alter call.

The Rain of Love

In God's presence,
I kneel to pray
For my heart is burdened
With worries today.

In God's presence,
I'm upset and bold
For these heavy thoughts
Must be told.

I can feel
The Lord is near
As I lower my head
And wipe a tear.

The elegant words
I wanted to say,
They would not come
As I knelt to pray.

But in my soul,
A peacefulness grew
As I could feel
God's light shine through.

My thirsty mind
Was quenched again
By God's love
That fell like rain.

The burdens are lifted
And all grows still
As in God's presence,
I receive His will.

A Call for Help

God bless you in sorrow,
Let the sadness drift away,
May His love uphold you
Through the coming day.

When you feel let down,
Search for comfort from pain,
These questions you ask,
He will visit once again.

There is no holding back
When you kneel in prayer
For the Lord will hear you
'Cause He's always there.

When those teardrops fall
And your torment is real,
God will answer you,
No matter how you feel.

His door is always open,
Take the courage to walk through,
God is waiting there –
'Cause He has time for you.

The Flight to Paradise

Out of the depths
Of each empty soul,
We ask, heavenly Father
To make us whole.

Shine into the corners
Where we hide afraid
And acknowledge to all
That Christ will save.

Wash us anew
In Your Spirit divine
For we sing a new song
Of that glorious time.

With hearts full of joy,
In thanksgiving we sing,
These praises of love
To Jesus, our King.

Then on golden wings
Of angels we fly
To Your paradise
Somewhere in the sky.

There we can bow
In grateful praise,
To sing out in joy –
Glad voices we raise.

Call Out to You

Lord, we pray for the sick,
The tormented and lame,
We cry out to You
In our moment of shame.

We ache for the hungry,
The children in pain,
We call out to You, Lord,
Now, hear us again.

Bless the downtrodden
And those all alone,
We call out to You, Lord,
To give them a home.

For their struggle in darkness,
A plate with no food,
We cry out to You, Lord,
Help us do some good.

When all seems forsaken
And man stands at a loss,
We call out to You, Lord,
Remembering the cross.

We cry out to You, Lord,
What more can we do
To show our lost brothers
The way home to You?

Off to See Jesus

Winging to heaven,
Our souls take flight,
Off to see Jesus
In His glorious light.

Life's journey now ended,
The victory is won,
Off to see Jesus
Up past the sun.

How we have waited,
Longing to be
Off to see Jesus
And pray at His knee.

Gone from our families,
Many friends we have left,
Off to see Jesus
Was our parting gift.

Hope upon hope,
A new life has begun,
Off to see Jesus,
Our struggle is done.

How very sad
Was that final goodbye,
Off to see Jesus
In the sweet by and by.

Don't cry for us
Or ring the death bell,
We're off to see Jesus –
Come bid us farewell.

To Mend a Hurt

This world, it tempts us
And troubles each heart
But in God's grace,
We find a new start.

Lift joyful voices
To God in praise,
Sing out, sing out
In these final days.

Come rest your soul
At His mercy seat,
These moments of peace,
You may now keep.

Oh, dare yourself
To pray out loud,
Come lift your songs
Above the cloud.

There is no fright,
No hidden pain
For our Lord, Jesus
Can heal again.

Come steal away
Beyond shadowed doors
For He waits to mend
Your hurts and sores.

The Cup of Grace

Come quench your thirst
And dry your tears,
God fills this cup,
He is right here.

No need to languish
And go without
As His cup of grace
Is passed about.

Oh, weary heart,
Do not complain,
The Holy Spirit
Soothes your pain.

He fills your cup
With saving grace
And encourages you
To win life's race.

The cup of love
Returns once more,
Sip from the brim
As you did before.

Come feed from God,
Oh, lift your cup
And thank our Saviour
As you sup.

Flower of Peace

The flower of peace
Blooms brightly today,
Partake of its goodness,
Chase worries away.

Smell the fragrance of glory,
Breathe it deeply in,
Respond to the nudging
That's created by Him.

Flower of peace –
I feel in my mind
The need to surrender,
You are quite divine.

Your blossoms open wide
For this world to see,
How inviting you are
For each hungry bee.

For God in His wisdom
Has captured His grace
In that smile of beauty
That glows on your face.

Oh, flower of peace,
Your petals so soft
Float into the air
And are carried aloft.

Yes, carried to heaven
To lay on the path
Where man will be free
From the devil's wrath.

Our Patient Teacher

He covers us with His feathers
And guides us to heaven's gate,
We needn't worry or stumble
Or wonder about our fate.

God baptizes at the pool
Where living waters flow
And fills us with His love
So fully that we glow.

God's blessings we feel,
Our souls he has reformed
As His refining fire
Melts away the scorn.

He teaches us with patience
Keeping no track of time,
Pouring out His grace
To fill each heart and mind.

Being more humble,
Come bow at His feet
And offer your praises
At His mercy seat.

Give God the glory
And our love so true
For how His precious Son
Forgave me and you.

Talk It Out

Don't sit on your chair
And play peek-a-boo
Waiting for God
To look down on you.

Get with the program,
Reach out to Him,
Pray now in earnest
From deep within.

Muster up courage,
Tell God your thoughts,
Talk to this Friend,
Just as you ought.

Don't wait for tomorrow,
Don't putter and scoff,
Those fetters that bind you
Won't have fallen off.

Don't play peek-a-boo
And wander about,
Get down to business
With God – work it out.

He has your number,
Don't sit back and snooze,
Come talk it all out –
There's no to time to lose.

The longer you talk,
The smaller problems will be,
Don't pay a shrink
'Cause with God, it's free.

Wretched Human

Oh, wretched human,
That I be,
There is no compassion
That comforts me.

No loving touch
Or strong arm,
No words of wisdom
To keep from harm.

No caring handshake
Or friendly smile,
No one to listen
For just awhile.

Oh, wretched human,
That I be,
Why have they all
Withdrawn from me?

What have I lost?
Oh, can it be
The flame went out
And I do not see?

I stand alone
Ashamed and blue,
My friends are gone,
They've come to You.

Oh, wretched human
That I be,
God will You hear
And forgive me?

Carried on High

Heavenly Father,
We call out to You,
Come lift the burdens
That tear us in two.
Fill up our souls
With Your heavenly light,
Baptize these children
With Your gracious might.
We worry and stumble
When life grows dim,
Searching for love
That comes only from Him.

Angels surround us
To carry us high
Meeting our Father
There in the sky.
We sing out these praises
Knowing we'll meet
With Jesus, our Saviour,
Our voices grow sweet,
Then to be carried
Up and away
With You, our Saviour
On this glorious day.

Walk Not Alone

You see me stand alone,
In a crowd I might be
But never alone am I
Because Jesus walks with me.

It is your choice to make,
Draw God to Your side,
Invite Him as your Friend,
Don't turn your back and hide.

Purge Us Again

Don't be alone
For there is time
To ask the Saviour
Come and refine.

So pitiful be
Your humble cry,
Call out to God
Up in the sky.

Purge us again
To start anew
And claim that promise
He walks with you.

For there will be
In glory days,
A song to sing
Of heavenly praise.

Meeting Jesus

I rush down the path
Going to see
This new teacher
From Galilee.

I am so excited
As onward I dash –
Where is this Jesus?
I go in a flash.

They say He's majestic –
Not dressed like a King
And when He speaks,
How His words ring.

Oh, what a joy,
My heart's burning like fire,
I want only to touch –
It is my desire.

Reaching and stretching
Straining to be
One innocent child
Just wanting to see.

Suddenly my fingertips
Brush something soft
And my little heart –
It is carried aloft.

The peace, how it flooded
From head to my toes,
My inner being
Just started to glow.

The joy bubbled up
And it consumed me.
What is this feeling
That sets my soul free?

Then precious Jesus,
He stopped and He looked,
My little body,
It trembled and shook.

"Be not afraid
And come unto me,
As Father loves Son,
I also love Thee."

"But I am not worthy
Your child to be!"
I stammered softly,
"Can You forgive me?"

Then smiling and whispering
Down into my ear,
"I'm only too happy
To walk with you here."

Earthly Visitors

We are only visitors
And one day will be
Transported on high
And then set free.

No need to worry,
To languish from pain,
We'll walk with our Saviour
When He comes again.

We will travel
The streets paved in gold
And sing new songs
That are so bold.

We are blessed
And can some day
Dance with the angels
Then sing and pray.

Rejoice, rejoice
For we are told
That up in heaven
Are prophets of old.

All that we question
And wonder why,
Will be shown to us,
Now do not cry.

Hold fast to your faith
And do not give in,
For God's Holy Spirit
Now dwells within.

The Lonely Man

Oh, lonesome man
Who cannot see
That love of God
Will set him free.

He does not walk
The path of faith
To have his heart
Filled with God's grace.

And lower still,
He does not care
To come to Christ
In humble prayer.

Oh, lonely man
About to die,
There is still time
For him to cry.

To ask our Father
Who dwells above
To send His Spirit
And fill him with love.

In time of weakness
He must be strong,
Ask for forgiveness
To right the wrong.

Then in the flicker
Of his eye
He feels the presence
Of God nearby.

So as his life
Draws to its end,
He will know,
God is his friend.

Voices of Praise

Come to the cross,
Lift voices in praise.
Come sing hosannas,
Your glad hearts to raise.
Sing of the Saviour
And His love for you,
Sing of the valleys
He's carried us through.
Thanks to the Spirit
For covering each sin
And coming to dwell
Deep down within.

Be ever so thankful
For the path we walk
For blessings and comfort –
The joy we can talk.
Thank You, dear Father,
For Your loving pardon
And for the healing
In Your precious garden.
We lift voices of praise
For the vision we face,
Thank You for the blessings
Of Your saving grace.

Halleluiah Chorus

Oh, that we should praise you
For our daily bread
And offer up thanksgiving
From each humble head.

Our songs so full of glory
With voices always sweet,
Dwelling on Your holiness
When some day, we'll meet.

Your grace, we take for granted,
Knowing You are near
But never reaching out to You
Until we shed a tear.

But now we are aware
Of Your love sublime,
So fill our empty hearts
With Your Spirit fine.

God, hear our grateful voices,
This chorus that we raise,
Because our joy is lifted
In this new song of praise.

A Halleluiah chorus
Carried on angels' wings,
This song to You, our Father,
We are so glad to sing.

Something for Everyone

The books of the bible,
They really hold –
Something for everyone,
So we are told.

Keep an open mind
And read it so slow,
Study those verses,
The ones you don't know.

Do you see your problems
Set in another time
And is there an answer?
We'll read another line.

The slaves and the prophets
Are tempted and tried,
Just like today,
Mess up and you're fried.

The road has detours,
It snakes around the bend,
If you're not careful,
It means a sorry end.

But there is help,
Guide posts show the way,
You needn't walk alone,
As you travel today.

The Lord sent prophets,
Then His beloved Son –
No one ever promised
The trip would be fun.

But waiting in the lines,
The Spirit takes your hand,
Oh, what a comfort
To walk the narrow strand.

Do not be dismayed,
You're not the only one
To be helped along
By God's precious Son.

Vanquished Goal

I walked the road
Of lonely men
In search of God –
I looked for Him.

But in my haste
To go this day,
I could not find
Him anyway.

Instead I saw
The fields of green,
Is this where God
Might have been?

Then I saw
The lilies bright,
Reflecting all
His glorious light.

I smelled the fragrance
Of the pine
And marveled at chestnuts
Standing in line.

I heard the voices
Of birds so sweet
And tasted berries
Which were a treat.

Then I realize
This world abounds
With the presence of God
That is around.

In the midst
Of some vanquished goal
I know the Lord
Has blessed my soul.

Being Prepared

Are you prepared to go
Down the dusty way?
Are you ready to follow
Jesus Christ today?

Does temptation take you
On a murky detour?
Can you find your way back
Or are you unsure?

Are you committed
To travel with this man?
So are you prepared
To take His guiding Hand?

Do not be dismayed,
It is up to you
To follow in His footsteps
And keep from being blue.

God will let you choose
The way you want to go,
It's between the two of you
If you didn't know.

But if you decide
To go the other way,
God will welcome you home
On any given day.

The Narrow Way

Slowly down
The narrow way
Walks a solitary Man
And glowing from
His peaceful Face,
I reach to touch His Hand.

Then filled in awe,
I feel the surge
Rush into my soul –
For in the back
Of my racing mind,
I know He made me whole.

Oh, troubled soul,
Don't linger there
But come the narrow way,
Repent of deeds
That scar your life,
Hear what Jesus has to say.

He speaks of love
And forgiving sin,
Then patiently explains
Of a spiritual holiness
That comforts
Hurts and pains.

Do not fear,
Come honour Him,
Hear the song that's sung,
For in His word
We understand
That He and God are One.

Remembering Nan

A life fulfilled,
She is gone today
But in our hearts,
Glenda will stay.

A crocheted throw
Upon her knee
Nan rests peacefully
We can see.

A grandmother's dream –
Two girls and two boys,
The years you've brought
Her so much joy!

How she would laugh
When on her lap
You rode down the hall
Before a nap.

The years slipped by
She watched you grow
And when Glenda spoke
Her pride would show.

She sat and read
So we are told
At her favourite window
To the world.

To watch the deer
And chipmunks play,
The foxes and rabbits
Made her day.

All the fun you shared
At Christmas time
And your birthday gifts
Were just sublime.

But now she's gone
Our hearts grow sore,
These memories
We cherish forevermore.

September 9, 2013

A Compassionate Friend

Do you have a friend
Who is always there
When you're in need,
With whom you can share?

Do you have a friend
You can go to
When lonely and scared,
Feeling troubled and blue?

Do you have a friend
Who shows you the way
When everything goes wrong
On any given day?

Do you have friend
Who dwells in your heart
And gives you a nudge
When it's hard to start?

Do you have a friend
Who forgives and forgets
With no strings attached
That isn't a threat?

Well, open your bible
And you will find there,
A friend who is loving,
Compassionate and fair.

A friend who won't leave you
When the going gets tough
Who blesses and feeds you
With all the right stuff.

There's no need to worry
Or feel ashamed
For on Calvary's tree,
This Friend bore the blame.

Sweet Mercies

Joyful blessings
Grace my thoughts
As God's goodness
I have sought.

Forget the time
That I once lived
Because my Father
Can forgive.

And this heart,
It skips a beat
When I remember
His mercies sweet.

Now I lift
This grateful song
To sing His praises
All day long.

Oh, blessed King,
I sing to Thee
And thank You now
For saving me.

Jesus Came A-Knocking

When Jesus came a-knocking
At my heart's door,
I didn't have the patience
To cross the wooden floor.

What a day of shame,
I turned Him away
Not interested in anything
That He had to say.

But Jesus is persistent,
He caught me right off guard,
That day He came a-knocking
Out there in the yard.

His tender voice whispered,
I melted to my toes,
What day He comes a-knocking –
No one ever knows.

Now, I must admit,
His Spirit flooded in
And changed my way of thinking
From feet up to my chin.

All the time I've wasted,
Those years I've shut Him out
But Jesus came a-knocking –
He has a lot of clout.

There is no time to lose
For all I must take in
'Cause Jesus came a-knocking,
Now I'm gladly serving Him.

I have no time for dreaming
Complaining's passed me by
For Jesus came a-knocking
And I'm singing in the sky.

The Phone Call

Hello! Can You hear me?
I need to talk with You,
My best friend just died,
My heart is broken in two.

I hope I'm not intruding
On You this way,
I don't know what to do
And the things I should say.

Can You send some comfort
And a little love?
I am sure that You're listening
From Your throne above.

I don't often call
Or send thanks Your way
But because I'm sad,
I thought it's time to pray.

My neighbour says that she
Calls You every day
To chat about her worries –
You hear what shc has to say.

Now I'm glad I called,
Already I feel better,
Should I send a card
Or maybe write a letter?

Can I call again
Just to talk with You?
Thanks again for listening,
Now I don't feel so blue.

A Song of Joy

Lord, we search often
For Your saving grace,
Bowing in prayer
And renewing our faith.

Lord, we sing often
Your songs of praise
With voices of joy
In gratefulness we raise.

Lord, we seldom cry
For nothing is in vain
As Your healing touch
Removes our hurt and pain.

We know You hear us,
All singing aloud,
Songs of thanksgiving
Lifting up through the clouds.

Lord, we grow in Your wisdom,
Are filled with Your love,
Raising voices of joy
To You up above.

Lord, we sing out these songs
Offering You glory this way
For the compassion You shower
On Your children today.

A Gentle Dove

Help us, Lord,
To bow in prayer
And intercede
Because we care.

Then help us, Lord,
To say thank You
For all the blessings
That flow from You.

For we know,
On us the shame
Will multiply when
We ignore Your Name.

When in haste,
We do not pray
Words to intercede
For loved ones today.

We don't confide
Our inner fears
Or show compassion
For a stranger's tears.

Lord, pick us up
When we trip and fall
For we cannot hear
The needy call.

Lord, make us aware
Of Your spiritual love
And pass it around
Like a gentle dove.

Christmas Bells

Ring out – ring out,
Christmas bells,
Let us know
That all is well.

A child is born,
Oh, glorious day,
Who will take
Our sins away.

Make haste to see
This miraculous birth
That changes all
Who walk the earth.

As wise men three
Paid homage there
To show the world
That they care.

And humble though
The stable be,
Shepherds came
To worship Thee.

Ring out – ring out,
Oh, Christmas bells,
This joyful story
That you tell.

Our Heavenly Father

Lord, the road of life
Can be rough and steep,
We struggle at times
Through mud that is deep.

Then in our turmoil,
We turn to You,
Who is patiently waiting
To carry us through.

When hunger defeats us,
You feed us Your love
Sent by the angels
From heaven above.

When we are bogged down
By burdens in life,
It's Your Holy Spirit
That conquers our strife.

Oh, Wonder of all,
Such beauty and grace,
We have nothing to fear
In all that we face.

For You are our strength,
The Creator of all,
Who answers each prayer
When sadly we call.

To You, heavenly Father,
Goes all glory and songs
As from thankful hearts
You've forgiven our wrongs.

To You, heavenly Father
Who is triumphant in all,
Thank You for helping
Each time that we fall.

A Call to Prayer

A desperate voice calls
From humanity's sea,
"Can you help –
Will someone help me?"

What did God expect –
My brother's keeper to be?
Must I plunge into
That human sea?

As time grows short
And day is done,
What can I do
When a battle's won?

My money is gone,
The cupboard is bare,
How can I help
Those out there?

I hear the voice,
Oh, sadly plead,
What's left to give
To fill his need?

So call to God
In faithful prayer
And ask Him
To help out there.

Hope is not lost
To those who fall
When we can make
That prayer call.

Tender Mercies

Tender mercies
Flood over me
When I reach out
In need of Thee.

Mending this heart
And hurting mind,
Your consolation
I can find.

When the turmoil
Finally stills,
My empty soul
Your Spirit fills.

In humble prayer,
I search above
To ask forgiveness
And Your love.

For through faith,
Each battle that's won
Is a victory from
God's only Son.

Tender mercies
Flood over me
As I lift my praise
To honour Thee.

Humble Pie

Don't shout out
In boastful pride
But steal away
As if to hide,
Don't look around
Just to see
If someone watches
Filled with envy.
Go in prayer,
You can try –
Hunt for God's Ear,
Not someone's eye.

For humbleness grows
In a quiet place
To strengthen faith
In trouble we face.
So… bow your head
And quietly say
Your needs to God
Whenever you pray.
Alone with God,
Away from eyes,
Pray often to Him
And eat humble pie.

Starlight

A lonely star
Lights midnight's way
To a dark stable
Where Jesus lay.

With calves and lambs
In shining light,
Fullfilling prophecy
This holy night.

Kings from afar
Paid homage there
And brought Him gifts
To show they care.

Humble shepherds
Bow in the night
To babe in manger
'Neath star so bright.

Oh, star so bright,
You light the way
To the manger
Where He lay.

Then condemned –
No light in the sky,
He hangs on the cross
About to die.

Oh, lonely star,
You hide your face,
Not wanting to see
What's taking place.

From the tomb,
A light does shine
As Jesus leaves
It all behind.

In the heavens,
Brilliant lights glow
As the Master waits
For us to go.

Lifting Spirits

When day is done
And spirits sunk low,
Lord, lift us up
And make us glow.

When day is done
And we've grown weak,
Strengthen our hearts
In all we seek.

When day is done,
We praise and thank You
For every blessing
Poured out by You.

When day is done
And we are worn out,
There is still time
To talk things out.

In humble prayer,
We bow to Thee
For victories won
That sets spirits free.

When day is done,
We come Your way
To thank You, dear Father,
For loving us today.

Over the generations,
How happy we'll be,
When at day's end,
Prayers are heard by Thee.

Passing of a Friend

You had such a love for God,
We saw it in your eyes,
How often that you spoke of Him
Until the day you died.

You showed your love in charity
Helping everywhere you could,
Donating to the needy
And visiting those you should.

We listened when you spoke of God
And often heard you pray,
Infectious was God's love you had –
We felt it every day.

Now you've left this little flock
We often think of you,
We long to hear that gentle voice
Comforting us when we're blue.

One day, we hope to see you walk
Upon the distant sand
To see your face and hear your laugh
When we reach to shake your hand.

Songs of Love

Lowly and meek,
This carpenter's Son
Conquered the cross
On which He'd hung.

Leaving the tomb
For heaven on high
To live with His Father
Up in the sky.

Great battles fought,
Our Saviour won,
Now, do not reject
God's only Son.

Through His forgiveness,
Our voices, we raise,
Happily singing
Our songs of praise.

Sing out the words
That we understand,
Words that are simple
From mortal man.

Overflowing with peace,
Lift songs of love
Filled with thanksgiving
To heaven above.

An Advent Prayer

Heavenly Father, teach us patience
In our prayers of forgiveness during Advent.
We lean on the promise of the filling
Of Your spiritual grace.
Continue to keep Your children humble
In our tasks, knowing our daily witness
Reflects the love we have for Christ Jesus.
Teach us to be more understanding
Of our fellow man and to be less hypocritical
Of the actions of those around us.
It is not us who should judge others
But be loving, and treat each other
As You, Lord, love us.
Thank You for hearing our prayers
In this Advent season,
We ask in Jesus' Name.

Amen

In God's Sanctuary

A church's sanctuary today is like
The early temples' holiest of holies.
God has given us the privilege
To enter into this holy place with Him every Sunday.
Here we can partake of the spiritual feast
Jesus has prepared for us.
When we are absent from this sanctuary –
God provides His Holy Spirit to dwell
Inside of us to provide comfort
And guidance in our lives.
We truly are blessed and enriched
Through this relationship with our God.
We are comforted by the presence of His grace
And because of God's grace, each man
Is a sanctuary unto himself.

Truth

No word is larger
Or more sublime
Than God's love
That is divine.

No promise made
To man from above
Will be greater
Than God's love.

When we search for truth
In fervent prayers,
The answer comes
To show He cares.

Come share the truth
So all can see,
How much God's love
Can set us free.

His truth will cleanse us
All from sin
And fill empty hearts
Up to the brim.

The truth of life
That God can give
Will teach us all
How we can live.

Understanding Grace

I understand the evening star
Shining, oh, so bright,
Casting light on Bethlehem,
It made a holy night.

I understand His years of youth,
Even way back then,
Gathering wisdom from the minds
Of the learned men.

And the wonder of the day
When John baptized, we see
A filling by the spiritual dove
To set this young Man free.

I understand the gathering
Of a band of men
And how He taught with loving care
To all who listened in.

But it hurts my saddened heart
When hanging on the cross,
He gave up His life on one cruel day
So man would not be lost.

I understand the empty tomb
For Jesus wasn't there,
He's sitting at His Father's throne
Somewhere in the air.

I understand how he suffered
But it's hard to see
Why Jesus died the way He did
For the likes of me.

Godly Grace

Oh, that I,
More humble be
To seek Your glory
Which fills me
And in time
Of dire greed,
Reach out to You
And fill my need.
I bow to You
Each day and pray
With all the things
I need to say,

To search for You
In all I see
And be thankful
That You love me,
Then walk Your way
In sheer delight
To be renewed
By all Your might,
For I know
And am aware
That through grace,
You really care.

A Psalm of Thanksgiving

With thanksgiving and joy,
We bow to Thee
To offer our praises
On bended knee.

We sing and dance
To You on high
Because You listen
Whenever we cry.

You feel our hurts
And inner fears
Then wipe away
Our sudden tears.

You build us up
And don't let us down
Then walk with us
On higher ground.

Whenever we stumble
And start to fall
Lord, it is You
To Whom we call.

In the early
Light of dawn,
It is to Your Spirit
That we are drawn.

The Invitation

When His living waters
Flood within your soul,
Know it is our Saviour
Who will make you whole.

He will cleanse your being,
Set you free of sin
But you must invite
Him to come within.

Do not hesitate
And put Him off,
Time is growing late,
Come to the feeding trough.

He can fill your longing,
Take you by the hand
Guide you through the rough spots –
Alone, you need not stand.

Come to God for comfort,
Do not turn away,
He's waiting there to help you,
Depend on Him today.

Together you will conquer
Every trial you find,
You will never falter –
He won't leave you behind.

Do not turn away,
His door is open wide,
God loves us as we are,
There is no need to hide.

Accept His invitation,
Do not be so blue,
Come live with God,
Feel how He loves you.

Old Noah

Old Noah set out
Just in time
To build a boat
That's mighty fine.

When the rains
Came tumbling down,
Noah and family
Were dry and sound.

His neighbours mocked
And laughed at him,
They thought it was
A silly whim.

Upon the water
Went that boat,
Yes, forty days,
They did float.

Well, Noah gathered
From around,
All the animals
That could be found.

Then one day,
The rains did stop,
Boat came to rest
On a mountaintop.

They filled that boat
In every space,
You could see
It lit up his face.

Old Noah laughed
And jumped with glee –
He let the animals
All go free.

Noah built an alter
On the ground
To thank the Lord
For being safe and sound.

The Passion of Christ

Remember His passion
At the cross,
That sacrifice made
Will not be lost.

Tear down God's temple,
It was built up
In just three days,
Jesus was lifted up.

The miracles were many
In Galilee
And even when Jesus
Sat by the sea.

The multitudes,
They came to eat
His spiritual feast
As well as the meat.

How Jesus suffered,
He bled and died
There on the cross
Where we all cried.

But do not weep,
God is here today,
Come pray to Him –
Wipe your tears away.

A Sunday Prayer

Heavenly Father,
Anoint us with Your presence
That we might call out to You
In adoration and praise.
Renew a right spirit in our hearts
As we lift grateful voices
Of joy to You.
Lord, in all things, increase
Our need to lean on You
And remain humble in our faith,
Seeking forgiveness for our sins
And strength through Jesus' blood
For our weaknesses and shortcomings.
Help us, Father, to be ever constant
In our prayers and our songs of glory.
We ask in Your loving Name.

Amen

Thankful Confession

Hear this cry
For mercy, Lord,
Can You set me free
As I bow in humbleness,
Do You hear my plea?

In my tribulation
And trials that I face,
It's You, my Father
To whom I come
To seek more of Your grace.

In these hours of turmoil,
I call upon Your Name
Because, in weakness
And temptation,
You take away the shame.

I sing to You,
These praises, God,
You're always by my side
When I blindly stumble
And have nowhere to hide.

With patience, I can wait
At Your mercy seat
Then walk to
Your blood-stained cross
On these trembling feet.

You are a God of mercy,
Your compassion shines
And in this hour of need,
Now I confess
That you are mine.

Wasted Years

It took a lot of courage,
To get down on your knee,
To ask the Lord, in reverence,
Just to set you free.

The years that were wasted –
Those, I cannot count,
The troubles I endured
Are too hard to surmount.

What was the final blow
That caught you right off guard,
To bow before our Father
That you found so hard?

Forgiveness now, is golden,
His love it survives,
Because of the cross,
Grace won't be denied.

Filled with God's love,
Your burden is gone,
Sing out to others
With a new song.

Sing out with joy,
Clap hands in pride,
Words to your new song,
No longer will hide.

Up to the heavens,
Choir voices now sing,
Words of this new song,
In glory will spring.

Breath of God

Walk in the wind
It's the breath of God,
Stirring His people
Where Jesus once trod.

Come for a filling
In heart and in soul,
Walk in His breath
And become whole.

Bow down in prayer
At His mercy seat,
Wait for the breeze
That is tender and sweet.

Feel His warm breath
Sweep over the land,
Come and be touched
By God's loving Hand.

His Spirit, like wind,
Sweeping the ground,
Loosening the fetters
From all who are bound.

Forgiving and renewing
All who are lost,
Purchased at Calvary,
Remember the cost.

"Wait for the wind,"
Whispers this breeze
As it stirs within you
Down on your knees.

The Master Spoke

The Master spoke
So all could hear,
"Come much closer
And do not fear."

"I speak to one
And then to all,
Live by My word
And do not fall."

"For My Son
Called out in strife
To give you all
Eternal life."

"And hanging on
That dreadful tree,
Gave up the fight –
To set us free."

The Master spoke
With gentle love
And I heard His angels
Sing above.

Do not weep,
For God's Son,
The battle's over
And victory's won.

Tell His story,
Sing out and cheer
So all may know
That God is near.

Tell your children
Of God's love,
Then send thanks
To Christ above.

Cower in Fright

I search for peace
Throughout my day,
Your Spirit fills me
Along the way.

Help me to walk
The narrow way,
Then provide the words
I need to say.

Give me the strength
To bow in prayer
And with humble voice,
To say I care.

When it's dark
And I cower in fright,
I ask You, Lord,
To shine Your light.

So that my work
And witness true
Reflects the praise
I give to You.

For it's You I know
And boldly say,
Have changed my life
In a precious way.

About Face

About face
Is what we did
To hear how our Saviour
Suffered and bled.

A whip on the back,
Thorns on His Head,
The nails and a spear –
Now He is dead.

With broken hearts,
We wail in pain,
The Saviour is gone
Is our sad refrain.

Oh, terrible day,
How can it be,
Jesus is taken
From you and me?

Afraid to speak out,
We turn our backs,
Sadly walking
Down the tracks.

The news has come,
Oh, praise the day –
The tomb is empty,
Its stone rolled away.

Jesus is risen,
We cry aloud,
Joining His Father
Above the clouds.

Oh, happy day
In the upper room,
He came to them
Out of the gloom.

To pass God's love
And His Spirit on,
Then in a twinkle,
He was gone.

About face
Is what we did,
For Jesus is with us –
He is not dead.

Journey of Life

I reached that spot
In the journey of Life
When I couldn't find comfort
For my worry and strife.

I was lost in the dark,
Knowing not what to do,
Feeling sorry for myself
Made my heart blue.

In that hour of need,
I cried aloud,
Asking forgiveness,
I humbly bowed.

Then came such a peace
Like a burning fire,
Hold onto this moment,
Was my only desire.

Why hadn't I felt
Like this before?
Well, I'd never knocked
On God's prayer door.

Life's journey is different,
The things that I face
Aren't quite the same
Now filled with God's grace.

Now I can walk
As one joyful man
In the shadow
Of God's loving Hand.

Showers of Blessing

We do not stand
In soaking showers
To hang our heads
Like drooping flowers.

We bow humbly,
Hungrily asking
For God to send
His showers of blessing.

Wash us anew,
Remove our fright,
Unlock the fetters
That are so tight.

Pour over us
Your Spiritual love
To comfort all
From Your throne above.

We may raise
Our voices high
With joyful words
Sent to the sky.

Come sing with us
Songs of thanksgiving
Because showers of blessing
Are what God is sending.

At Some Future Time

Tiny hands folded
Beside his bed,
Quietly kneeling
And bowing his head.

Softly asking God
To watch over him
Then to protect
His small brother, Jim.

He thanked God for parents
And grandparents, too,
Then asked his Father
For a pair of new shoes.

I fought back the tears
For my son's little prayer
And that innocent faith
In his moment of care.

This tender moment
I'll hold in my mind
To savour its sweetness
At some future time.

Burst Forth

Joyful women,
Six hundred strong,
Come together,
They can't be wrong.

With thankful hearts,
The speakers talk
Of life's trials
And their Godly walk.

Clap your hands
Or quietly hear
A gripping tale
To dispel your fear.

From across the country,
We see each face,
The shining light
Of God's grace.

Hug the strangers,
Shake their hands,
These Christian sisters
From distant lands.

Oh, come together,
Laugh and share
Four days of joy
Because God is there.

In colourful dress,
With songs of joy,
These cheerful voices
Do employ.

Our church isn't dead,
It does survive
As women gather,
Their faith comes alive.

Burst forth and tell
With love and glee,
Our church is alive
For all to see.

From every province,
Young and old,
These women gather –
A sight to behold.

It Could Not Last

It could not last
And now we fear,
Jesus is gone –
He is not here.

It could not last,
We felt His pain
In the hours of struggle,
We saw His strain.

His gentle voice,
We did not fear,
Jesus' patience
We all held dear.

His words, they sting,
Filling our minds,
Now we hold tight
To those precious times.

The thoughts of wisdom
And His healing touch,
The innocent children
That He loved so much.

The dusty road,
He slowly walked,
God's spiritual presence
When Jesus talked.

No minutes wasted,
His teaching prayers,
Forgiveness of sinners
Proved the Master cares.

In our memories
Of time past,
Christ is gone –
It could not last.

Softly Praying

I heard her praying all alone
Bowed in God's presence at His throne.

Phrases sweet and sincere
Her love of God made very clear.

Softly speaking to a friend
Conversation I hoped would not end.

Words of thanksgiving and praises, too,
Nothing fancy – that wouldn't do.

In that moment I became aware
Of God's peace that lingered there.

Filling heart and flooding soul
By His presence now made whole.

Yes, I heard her praying all alone
Then knelt beside her at God's throne.

Victory is Waiting

Climb Calvary's mountain
Where teardrops fall,
There Jesus died –
He gave His all.
Take the path to the tomb,
Stones are worn bare,
Look into that place
For He is not there.

Jesus went ahead
To prepare us a place
Where we can all live
In the light of His grace.
Forget about tomorrow,
It may never come –
That victory is waiting,
Now life's battle is won.

Under God's Hand

How I feel protected,
Sinner that I am,
For I'm safely covered
In the shadow of God's Hand.

Decisions are not difficult,
There is always light
For Jesus steals the darkness
To shine forever bright.

Turn away from folly,
Help's a prayer away,
So do not hesitate
Before you're led astray.

Beneath that outstretched Hand
Coming from above,
Feel the warming tenderness
That is called God's love.

No need to walk alone,
The time is never late
Asking His forgiveness,
Turn from devilish hate.

In the morning, you awaken,
You are not a lonely man
For today you walk with Jesus
'Neath the shadow of His Hand.

Compassion

When do we show compassion,
How often share our love?
Do we understand,
It comes from God above?

Can we share our table,
Learn we should not horde,
Food must not be wasted –
Wealth comes from the Lord?

It's time to teach our children
The importance of God's call,
Sharing with our brothers
Is the gift given to us all.

Don't look the other way,
Compassion shouldn't end,
Share it with a stranger,
A brother or a friend.

The greatest gift is love –
Jesus gave His all,
Can we begin to give,
To share and not to fall?

It's written in God's word
That hatefulness and strife
Can be overcome by
The promise of eternal life.

Heavenly Treasures

We bow in the graciousness
Of our eternal King,
Lifting glad voices,
We thankfully sing.

Oh, for the wonder
To us God has given
Fresh water and fishes
And treasures from heaven.

Love so divine,
No end do we see,
How does He feed us
And set us all free?

Come to God's cross,
Ask forgiveness of sin,
All will be lifted
And taken by Him.

He'll take your hand,
Lead you from strife,
Then walk along with you
The rest of your life.

Oh, bow to your Saviour,
Thank Him with love
As He pours down His glory
From His throne up above.

One Smile

Pray often to God
For I know very well;
It's all that keeps me
From the road to hell.

It's a constant job
I do every day;
To humble myself
Before God and pray.

Pray for His joy
And forgiveness, too;
Offer thanksgiving
For all that I do.

It isn't so bad –
A good habit I say,
To talk to the Lord
At the start of the day.

Then in the evenings'
Darkening hours,
I bow to thank God
For birds and the flowers.

Thank Him for entrusting
The jobs that I do
Here on this earth
To help those that are blue.

If I can put just
One smile on a face
And share with one person
Some of God's grace.

Then, thank You, Lord Jesus,
For giving to me,
A chance for setting
One person free.

Wisdom and Love

I am so humble
When I come to Thee
And ask you, Lord,
To forgive me.

Fill me, Lord,
With Your saving grace
To give me strength
For trials I face.

Pour out your wisdom
From up above,
Lord, thank You for
Your abundant love.

Thank You, Lord,
For taking my hand
For the times You carried me
Over the sand.

For all Your blessings,
So rich and kind
That's helped to settle
This contrite mind.

So when I come
To You in prayer,
Thank You, Father,
For being there.

God Cares

Lord, when I come
On bended knee,
I will praise
And honour Thee.

Lift You up
And praise Your name,
Call you Holy,
Understand Your fame.

Thank You, Lord,
For Your blessed Son,
For every victory
That He has won.

What grace You show,
All peace You give,
Because of You, Lord,
We so richly live.

So when I bow
And say a prayer,
I know You listen
And that You care.

Thank You, Father,
For hearing me,
For answering these requests
That I leave with Thee.

Prayer Time

Take the time
To bow in prayer;
Tell the Lord
How much you care.

Ask the Father
To set you free
From the turmoil
That shouldn't be.

Offer God thanks
And joyful praise
For the many blessings
Enjoyed these days.

Oh, come in prayer
To His mercy seat
And lay your burdens
At His feet.

Don't be shy;
Don't walk away;
Come to His table
To eat today.

Humble yourself
In urgent prayer,
Praise God and thank Him
For being here.

Amen

Praying for Guidance

Heavenly Father,
We surrender our hearts
And wills to You this morning.
We ask for Your abiding peace
And comfort for this day,
Lord, grant us humility
And grace to face any trials
Or temptations we may encounter.
Make us aware of the needs of those around us.
Free our minds of envy
And any slanderous thoughts,
Make us more thankful
Of blessings that come our way.
Help us to show kindness
And concern to neighbours
And loved ones.
Take away any arrogance
That might hinder us today.
Lord, make us
Thankful of the blessings
From Your Son and more aware
Of the presence
Of Your Holy Spirit
In all we think and do today.

We ask in Your loving Name.

Amen

A Prayer Shared

We come to Your throne,
Not with our cares
But offer the needs
Of others in prayers.

For those who lay sick
Upon their beds,
Send healing rain
To shower their heads.

For broken hearts
And stumbling minds,
Send Your encouragement
So loving and kind.

For orphaned children,
Hungry and scared,
We pray for their comfort,
Show them You care.

For those who are lost,
Don't know what to do,
Offer Your guiding Hand,
To come unto You.

Lord, thank You
For teaching us to share,
A way to help others
By coming in prayer.

Amen

Common Prayer

In the quietness of this hour,
We humble ourselves at Your mercy seat.
Make us instruments of Your grace.
Keep us mindful of the sacrifice
On Calvary's tree.
We pray for our government's decision-makers.
Give them wisdom and common sense.
Lord, we lift prayers of intercession
For health care workers, doctors
And law enforcement.
We pray that decisions made
Come through a concern
For the common good of all men,
No matter what the race or belief they have.
Teach us the need of intercessory prayer, Lord,
And the donation of time and care
For those less fortunate than ourselves.
Help us to build Your church,
Not destroy it through greed and pettiness.
Lord, give us loving hearts
And patient minds
To deal with our trials
As true children of God.
Teach us to step out in faith
And seek Your will in our lives.
We ask in Your loving Name.

Amen

Seeing God

I see God's grace
In each new tree
And hear His song
Sung by the bee.

I see His love
In every child
And playful games
As they run wild.

I see His patience
In yellow flowers
As their petals
Grace the bowers.

I see God smile
In the spring
When bursting buds
Begin to sing.

Then I see God cry
A salty tear
When hearts are wounded
By a spear.

I see His anguish
When we don't care
And never come
In humble prayer.

Then I see
His unwavering love
That descends from heaven
Like the dove –

To rest in every
Searching soul
Who ask of Him
To be made whole.

Faithful Prayer

Heavenly Father,
I bow in reverence
For Your grace,
Knowing full well,
Jesus took my place.
When He died
On Calvary's tree,
Those nail-pierced hands,
They bled for me.
Now I come
In humble prayer
And ask, dear Lord,
For continued care.

Throughout this day,
Control the things
That I will say.
Show Your mercy
One more time
As I clear
This sinful mind.
I ask for pardon
And renewed faith,
Raising my joyful
Voice to sing
Praises to You,
My coming King.

Amen

Death of Christ

Time, it will stop
Some mournful day
When dead on the ground,
You quietly lay.

We stand aghast,
Holding our breath,
We never thought of
Seeing You in death.

Ring out the bells,
We all repent
As our mournful voices
Sing this lament.

Together, hold hands,
Try to be brave,
Too soon You will travel
Off to the grave.

Go to the hilltop,
Look at the cross,
There it stands empty
Showing our loss.

But down in the tomb,
Your life is now spent,
We feel only sorrow
And deep discontent.

Oh, Master, come back,
We cry out to Thee,
See how humble,
We pray on bent knee.

"Come back to Your flock,"
We call out in love,
"Send down Your Spirit
From heaven above."

Heavenly Seed

We say a humble prayer
With our heads bowed low,
It is to our Saviour
Who has loved us so.

We pass on our thanksgiving
And many praises, too,
For we are so grateful
In the blessings from You.

It takes a lot of patience
Coming from this man
To guide His little children
With that outstretched Hand.

For we still are growing
And learning as we go
So heavenly Father –
Thank You
For all the seeds You sow.

Someday in the future,
We will understand
The fullness of God's love
When we reach the promised land.

A Donkey's Prayer

Little donkey,
I hear you cry
As down the path
You canter by.

A precious load
Upon your back,
I feel your pride
As you walk the track.

I understand God's favour
For picking this beast
To humbly carry Jesus
To His last feast,

Now in the light
Of future days,
I recognize the song –
When a donkey prays.

Well Done

At eventide
When dark has come,
I wait in prayer
To hear, "Well done."

I must admit
Through falling tear,
There was no answer
That I can hear.

A lack of effort
When I start,
Some unknown sin
Set me apart.

Then in meekness,
I bow to pray,
What careless thing
Have I done today?

What hurtful phrase
Or lack of love
Have I sent
To You above?

What troubled thought
Or negative word
Carelessly spoken
Have You heard?

Can You forgive
And set me free,
Then mould my will
How it ought to be?

So I might hear
Before the rising sun,
You lovingly whisper,
"My child, well done."

Come, Heavenly Father

Deep within my bosom
Anxiously crying out to Thee,
Remove this grievous feeling,
Come, Lord, set me free.

Teach us Your loving wisdom,
Words we long to hear,
Fill us with Your joy,
Fill us with Your cheer.

Remove all this heaviness
Felt by mortal man,
Fill us with Your kindness
In a sweep of Your hand.

We understand Your glory
In the agony Jesus faced,
Come, heavenly Father,
Fill us with Your grace.

Remove again the sadness
Of our troubled souls,
Come, heavenly Father,
Feed and make us whole.

Humble is He

In the dying
Light of day
Across the fields,
Hear him bray.

This rattling sound
That wakes the dead
And fills your mind
With so much dread.

For years old donkey
Had his say
And sang that song
At the end of day.

The butt of jokes,
There was no end,
Those floppy ears –
He had no friend.

But once upon
A glorious day,
Palm branches waved
As he came their way.

Oh, so soon
We have forgot,
The precious cargo
He carried aloft.

Walking Together

Each day we go a-walking
Through life's miry clay,
Hitting many detours
That can lead us astray.

When we go a-walking,
Sign boards we must read,
Take the time to stop
And then carefully heed.

Jesus points the way
Through life that we must go,
It is the right direction
Because He loves us so.

Where the water's deep,
Fear not my worried lass,
Jesus is the bridge
Now you can safely pass.

He calms the tempest blowing,
Then dries your salty tears
And in the darkest places,
We have nothing left to fear.

Come with me a-walking
For we are not alone,
We'll cross the clay together
And safely reach our home.

Working of the Spirit

I feel the Spirit's presence
Deep within my soul,
He lingers in my heart
Purging to make me whole.

The comfort of His nearness
Is a puzzle to me,
How He unlocks the secrets
To set this sinner free.

The working of His goodness
That forgiveness I adore –
The potter shaped the clay
Into a jug it wasn't before.

Heavenly Music

Nothing better
On earth is found
Than angels singing
Above the ground.

Burning verses
Sets hearts on fire,
Filling souls
Is God's desire.

Oh, blessed thought,
Praise the day,
When heavenly angels
Come your way.

Hear their song,
Come dance with me,
Heaven's music
Will set us free.

Clap your hands
In joyful praise,
Grateful voices
To God we raise.

For nothing's better
In hearts that are ringing
Than heavenly angels
Joyfully singing.

God's Wealth

We till the soil
And harvest Your crops,
Our thanksgiving to You
Will never stop.

You will not go unnoticed
In the jobs we do
For our praises are lifted
Joyfully to You.

Amen

Jesus Has Risen

Worship His majesty,
Sing to the Lord
For Jesus has risen
Fulfilling God's word.

From manger to cross,
From tomb to the sky,
Our precious Saviour
Is now up on high.

We stand in God's Spirit
And sing out our praise,
"Jesus has risen!"
Joyful songs we raise.

In My Own Way

With humble heart,
I pray to Thee,
"Thank You, Father,
For saving me."

With quiet voice,
I say out loud,
"Come once more
Upon Your cloud."

I come to ask
In my own way
And thank You, Lord,
For Jesus today.

May this time
I spend with You
Fill me with faith
And thankfulness, too.

May the forgiveness
Of all this sin
Be on my mind
When I pray to Him.

So thank You, Lord
And Spirit Divine
For filling my soul
With grace sublime.

Amen

Praying Together

Humbly we bow
Before Your mercy seat
Offering our prayers
At Your Holy Feet.

Can You now hear
Our prayers of passion
As together we raise
Requests in this fashion?

Asking for others
Who have lost their way
And for the confused
With no words to say.

We pray for the sick
The tormented and weak,
Asking You, Father,
Their needs You can meet.

Not for ourselves,
We pray up to Thee
But for the lost
Who need to be free.

Asking together,
Lord, hear our cries
Pour down Your blessings
So others don't die.

Hear our thanksgiving,
Our joyful songs raise,
Coming together
In glory and praise.

Rugged Tree

Oh, rugged tree
As you stand still,
Cry out to me
From Calvary's hill.

You are forlorn
Your wood is cold,
We feel your scorn
As it was told.

But know full well
When we ran to hide
That we must tell
Our Saviour died.

Oh, rugged tree,
God makes it known
When you call –
His love is shown.

For Jesus' pain
As He hung there
Was not in vain
Because we care.

Oh, rugged tree
We know so well,
The body you bore,
We can proudly tell.

Stained Glass

Flooding light
In coloured hues –
Yellows, reds
And dark blues.

Sunlight wafting
Rainbow strands,
Royal streams
That are grand.

Emitting colours
In shafts of light,
Dancing silent
And so bright.

Colours painting
Pew and floor,
Washing brightly
Near a door.

Royal purple
Crown of thorns,
Wooden cross,
Brown and forlorn.

Bethlehem's star,
Glowing white,
Beaming rays
Of heavenly light.

Sun-drenched windows
Through stained glass,
Glorious pictures
Of the past.

Mixing – mingling
On each seat,
Rays of colour –
A glorious treat.

The Book of Love

I am so humbled
By the stories I heard
That are written down
In God's holy word.

There were brave Christians
Who, once so shy,
Told stories of Jesus
Knowing they could die.

Of disciples who walked
Roads far from home
Preaching of God's grace
So brave and alone.

Of women in the background,
No powers to save,
Worshipped the Lord
Even at His grave.

Quiet people they were
But they could see
That great love of God
Would set them free.

Be it a Salome,
Ruth, Sarah or Mary,
Be it a Jonah,
John, Peter or Harry.

Of people so loving,
We read in this book –
Come open the cover
And have a good look.

Renewing Faith

Let the peace of Christ
In your heart reign,
Renew your faith,
Ask once again.

Let the Holy Spirit
Guide you today,
He's compass and roadmap
Along life's way.

Don't walk the path
In darkness alone
When God's precious light
Shines from His throne.

Don't let the pressure
Wear you down,
Be filled with God's Spirit –
Walk hallowed ground.

Come to the cross,
Kneel on bended knee,
Ask for His filling
And be set free.

Planting Seeds

Onto the dirt,
Each seed will fall
Fed by sun and rain
That covers all.

A little sprout
Begins to grow,
Someday we'll reap
Just what we sow.

The gangly twig
Must be nursed along
If it's to flower
And sing its song.

So strong young plant,
We can tell
You've been nourished
And are growing well.

For by God's Hand,
He brought you heat
And in your thirst,
Watered your feet.

So set your flowers
And bear your seed
To feed the hungry
Who are in need.

Holy Light

God's holy light
Shone all around
As eleven disciples
Knelt on the ground.

Hear reverent prayers
Being lifted on high
As trembling voices
Rose to the sky.

Do not give up
And don't lose sight
Of those sad men
Praying in holy light.

When in the midst
Of gloom and fear,
Jesus appeared
To dry every tear.

Come, Doubting Thomas,
Leave your thoughts behind,
Those nail-pierced hands
You now can find.

Come bend your knee
In darkest night
And pray to God
In His holy light.

Conversion

I prayed for conversion –
No lightning appeared,
Only a lifting
Of my fears.

I asked for forgiveness
Of many sins,
The heaviness left
From deep within.

I cried for God's Spirit
To live within
And felt a stir
Of a gentle wind.

What can this be –
When I have sought
These different changes
Christ has bought?

No lightning bolts,
No thunder rolls,
Just a nice warm feeling
From my head to my toes.

The dam didn't burst,
I never took flight
But stayed on my knees
Late into the night.

Three Nails

Three large nails
On the ground, they lay –
A stark reminder
Of that dreadful day.

Did poor blacksmith
At his forge so hot
Smite the steel
Really knowing not –

Those nails would hold
On wooden cross,
The sacrificial lamb that
Became the world's loss?

When the news
Spread around the town,
Did blacksmith bow
With a guilty frown?

And at his forge
On future days,
Were his nails smote
In a different way?

Beading on his brow,
The sweat fell like rain
To temper the steel
And hide his pain.

There on the ground,
Three nails lay
To remind this world
Of that dreadful day.

This Man — Jesus

We trembled in fear
And cried out to God,
Our Jesus is gone,
We have been robbed.

He had not finished
Teaching of love
That we all knew
Comes from God above.

Give us the strength
To carry on,
Show us your patience
Now Jesus is gone.

Fill us with wisdom
To lead others to You,
Provide bread and fishes
Feed the hungry, too.

Oh, come with Your love
And walk hand in hand,
Help your humble servants
Teach of this Man.

Family Grace

Father, we break this bread
Together as Your family,
We ask for peace and mercy
To nourish us as well.
As your family, Lord,
We lift our voices in thanksgiving
For all You give us.

Amen

Standing Together

We lost our friend
In the stormy deep,
Sadly we cry
Our broken hearts weep.

We wonder if you
Will ever return
Or are you lost,
Your soul to spurn?

We call out to God,
No answer does come,
Lost at sea –
No roll of the drum.

But we will wait
Here on the pier,
Praying your ship
Will sail in here.

We know that the sea
In anger lashed out
And finding your boat,
Tossed it about.

But people of faith
Will not give in,
And standing together
We all pray to Him.

Journey Home

Alas, my Saviour
Died for me,
Hanging alone
On Calvary's tree.

Oh, so lovingly
He gave life up
So this sinner
Could drink from His cup.

Now He waits
On distant shore
For His servant
To come once more.

I bow my head
In humble prayer
To tell my Saviour
I'm headed there.

To take my long
Awaited place
And stare so thankfully
Upon His Face.

God's Table

God answers prayer
When we are in need,
Come to His table –
There we can feed.

His saints and angels
Guide us along,
Teaching the difference
Between right and wrong.

Sing glory and praises,
The songs of His love,
Sing with His angels,
God's songs from above.

We needn't worry,
Be burdened with care,
Bowing in faith
We know that He's there.

Come to His table –
There we can dine,
The fruits of His love
Will be divine.

When we are filled
In every space,
We'll thank Him together
For His loving grace.

In the Shadows

He covers me
With His feathers
And I plainly see –
Leaning on my Saviour
Is the life for me.

His loving voice,
It teaches
What I need to know,
Then Jesus points the way
He wishes I must go.

Sometimes I disagree,
It is a human thing
But when I understand,
To Him my praises ring.

There are times I stumble
And weaken in His sight
But in the fear of darkness,
On me, God shines His light.

I tarry in the shadow
Of His precious Hand,
Knowing that He guides me
To the promised land.

Working Wonders

I get so mad at squirrel
For stealing the birds' feed,
Then I remember,
God made him to fill a need.

Well, God made me, too
And He works every day
At refining me
In His special way.

If I wasn't so stubborn
Life would go smoother, too,
But the Lord is patient
And He carries me through.

I am far from perfect
But it pleases me
That the lighted pathway
Is there to set us free.

Be it just a squirrel
And a sinner, too,
God will work His wonders
On folks like me and you.

Bountiful Harvest

For Your bountiful harvest
Thank You once more,
Heavenly Father,
Will You bless us as before?

We ask in Your loving name.

Amen

On Angel's Wings

On angel's wings,
I rode up high
Wondering if I
Was about to die.

I saw the heavens
Light up the sky
As ever higher,
We travelled nigh.

Up through the clouds
Of fluffy white,
I rode with my angel
Toward the light.

Oh, get prepared
To meet my fate
As life flashed before me –
The arrogance and hate.

Have I done enough,
Prayed through others' needs,
Helped where I could
And showed less greed?

Am I worthy to go
To the Holy Land
Or am I counted a failure
By mortal man?

God Visits Me

God visits me
When I'm cast down
And on my face,
I wear a frown.

God visits me
When in despair,
I bow my head
In anxious prayer.

God visits me
When once again,
I struggle with
A nagging pain.

He visits me
When bowed in prayer,
I promise Him
That I do care.

And God visits me
When I'm alone
And worry about friends
Who are far from home.

He visits me
When I can see,
It was His Son
Who set us free.

So when I come
In earnest prayer,
I thank my God
For being there.

Morning Hymn

Marching down the road
Comes a band of men
Joyfully singing
Their morning hymn.

Out in the meadow,
People crowd around,
That morning hymn
Is a joyful sound.

Up on the mount
At the empty tomb,
The morning hymn
Is a lovely tune.

That morning hymn
Is filled with love
As it gently rises
To heaven above.

The morning hymn
Fills each man's soul
And turns them from hate –
That is God's goal.

Down the path
And into town,
The morning hymn
Turns people around.

Come and sing,
Morning hymn with me
And let its words
Set your soul free.

Cry Out

Cry out – cry out
To God above,
He will send you
His infinite love.

Your fret and worry
Will not last
As you're guided by
The Shepherd's staff.

No need to face
Your trials alone,
Our God protects you
From His throne.

Burdens and worries
Will melt away –
God holds the answers
For you today.

Darkness wields
No powerful sway,
God's radiance shines
To light the way.

Cry out – cry out
In faithful prayers,
They will be heard
Because God cares.

Like the shepherd
From days of old,
God leads you gently
Into His fold.

God Has the Answer

He'll reach down His Hand
When you are blue –
God changes things
And will help you.

He hears what you say
And is your Friend,
God's love for you –
It has no end.

Walk not alone,
I gladly say,
God goes with you
Every day.

When you're cast down
Feeling nothing is right,
That is the moment
God shines His light.

You needn't worry
At what troubles you,
God has the answer
And knows what to do.

Blessings and grace,
He'll send your way,
God has the answer
To help you today.

Search for Joy

We can search everywhere
Feeling so blue
But, Lord, our peace
Comes only from You.

We can have riches
And at the same time,
Be poor in our hearts
Missing the sublime.

Thinking we're wise men
And knowing it all
But without Your wisdom,
We stumble and fall.

We can act pompous
Self-assured and so bold
But down in our hearts,
We're frigid and cold.

Search not for gold
And ill-fated gain
But look for God's love
And sing out His Name.

Then joy will come
As you praise Him each day
And be ever so thankful
That God came your way.

Jesus is Waiting

Jesus is asking,
"Come here to me."
He holds the answer
To set you free.

Free from life's burdens
And unknown sin
That you innocently hold
Deep down within.

Jesus is waiting,
A good Friend to be,
Waiting for you –
So come and see.

No questions asked,
Just unending love
Waiting with grace
That comes from above.

Jesus is wanting
To walk with you
Over rough ground –
He'll carry you through.

Forgiving and loving,
Then answering prayers,
Jesus is waiting –
See how He cares.

Jesus is smiling,
Can't you just see –
He's laid down His life
To set us all free.

Teach Me to Pray

Lord, please help me
Get this right,
I've worked all day
And half the night.

Can't You see
I've gotten behind,
This job is taxing me
Out of my mind.

Lord, please help
Give me the strength
To shop for groceries
And fill the gas tank.

Lord, give me the courage,
Just one more time
To tell a friend
What's on my mind.

Lord, can You give me
Extra time
To visit a while
With a sick aunt of mine?

Can You impose
Your loving will
To help my aunt
Who's been so ill?

Lord, can You help
At the end of the day
And teach me exactly
How I should pray?

For I know
I must thank You
For all the little
Things that You do.

When Things Go Amiss

God's love surpasses
Everything that we know,
Now come to listen,
He will tell you so.

God is very patient,
He understands
Weakness and hurt
Committed by man.

When things go amiss,
He will comfort you,
Forgiving the hateful
Things that you do.

That is His story –
Such infinite love,
Teaching in splendour
From heaven above.

What more could we want
From Spirit Divine,
Than some of His wisdom
For all mankind?

Guiding and helping,
Preparing the way,
For when we meet Jesus
On some future day.

No Greater Comfort

When I'm cast down,
Life's in disrepair,
Then I bow to Jesus
In earnest prayer.

No greater comfort
In life can there be
Than knowing that
My Jesus loves me.

Oh, troubled heart,
It doesn't take long
To understand
The right from wrong.

At the closing
Of every day,
Asking forgiveness
When I come to pray.

Then as I wait
On humble knees,
I hear Him whisper
Like a gentle breeze.

Oh, blessed Lord,
You cleanse my soul
And by Your grace,
I am made whole.

Retired Ministers

They shuffle to
Their favourite pews
In worn coats
And scruffy shoes.

With shining faces,
It is clear,
They hold this refuge
Very dear.

If called upon,
They bow in prayer
With eloquent words
To show they care.

Not like retirees
Who spend their time
In distant lands
With sun and wine.

With hearts beaming,
They do their best
And in retirement
Find needed rest.

So you can see
In their golden years –
Willingness to serve
With love and cheer.

Is There a Day?

Is there a hurt
You've not explored
Then brought your concern
To our dear Lord?

Is there a thought
Left unsaid
That fills the heart
With uneasy dread?

Or feelings hurt
By an innocent friend,
You won't let go
Until the end?

Is there a jab
In your mind –
You know is there
But cannot find?

Is there a day
Without a prayer
That Father God
May not be there?

Are you alone
And wonder why
No one listens
When you cry?

But all is well –
Just bow your head
And speak in faith
What needs to be said.

Knock on the door,
He will let you in
And share the love
That comes from Him.

Fallen Angel

A fallen angel
I wonder why,
A broken wing –
He cannot fly.

A fallen angel
With shameful face –
What has caused
His tumble from grace?

An angry word,
Oh, could it be,
A moment of weakness
Angel didn't see?

With broken heart,
He's gone astray,
So this fallen angel
Bows down to pray.

Then in the dark
God shines His light,
I quickly prayed
He'd make things right.

So now I see
Angel's little grin
It's welling up
From deep within.

Forgiveness defeats
And conquers all sin
So fallen angel
Can fly up again.

Alphabetical Index

Made in the USA
Charleston, SC
14 May 2015